COCAINE
AND CRACK

by James Barter

DRUG
EDUCATION
LIBRARY

Lucent Books, San Diego, CA
10911 Technology Place, San Diego, CA 92127

Library of Congress Cataloging-in-Publication Data

Barter, James, 1946–
    Cocaine and crack / by James Barter.
        p.   cm. — (Drug education library)
    Includes bibliographical references and index.
        ISBN 1-56006-912-0 (hard : alk. paper)
    1. Cocaine habit—Juvenile literature. 2. Cocaine—
Juvenile literature. 3. Crack (Drug)—Juvenile literature.
[1. Cocaine. 2. Crack (Drug) 3. Drug abuse.] I. Title.
II. Series.
    HV5810 .B37 2002
    362.29'8—dc21

2001001446

Copyright © 2002 by Lucent Books, Inc.
10911 Technology Place, San Diego, CA 92127
Printed in the U.S.A.

Contents

FOREWORD   4

INTRODUCTION
  The Cocaine Quagmire   6

CHAPTER ONE
  Cocaine: A Once-Promising Drug   10

CHAPTER TWO
  Illicit Use of Cocaine   23

CHAPTER THREE
  The Crack Epidemic   34

CHAPTER FOUR
  The Cocaine Partnership   50

CHAPTER FIVE
  Cocaine Interdiction   65

CHAPTER SIX
  Treatment and Recovery   80

EPILOGUE
  Is the Cost of the War on Cocaine Justified?   91

NOTES   94
ORGANIZATIONS TO CONTACT   98
FOR FURTHER READING   101
WORKS CONSULTED   102
INDEX   106
PICTURE CREDITS   111
ABOUT THE AUTHOR   112

Foreword

The development of drugs and drug use in America is a cultural paradox. On the one hand, strong, potentially dangerous drugs provide people with relief from numerous physical and psychological ailments. Sedatives like Valium counter the effects of anxiety; steroids treat severe burns, anemia, and some forms of cancer; morphine provides quick pain relief. On the other hand, many drugs (sedatives, steroids, and morphine among them) are consistently misused or abused. Millions of Americans struggle each year with drug addictions that overpower their ability to think and act rationally. Researchers often link drug abuse to criminal activity, traffic accidents, domestic violence, and suicide.

These harmful effects seem obvious today. Newspaper articles, medical papers, and scientific studies have highlighted the myriad problems drugs and drug use can cause. Yet, there was a time when many of the drugs now known to be harmful were actually believed to be beneficial. Cocaine, for example, was once hailed as a great cure, used to treat everything from nausea and weakness to colds and asthma. Developed in Europe during the 1880s, cocaine spread quickly to the United States where manufacturers made it the primary ingredient in such everyday substances as cough medicines, lozenges, and tonics. Likewise, heroin, an opium derivative, became a popular painkiller during the late nineteenth century. Doctors and patients flocked to American drugstores to buy heroin, described as the optimal cure for even the worst coughs and chest pains.

As more people began using these drugs, though, doctors, legislators, and the public at large began to realize that they were more damaging than beneficial. After years of using heroin as a painkiller, for example, patients began asking their doctors for larger and stronger doses. Cocaine users reported dangerous side effects, including hallucinations and wild mood shifts. As a result, the U.S. government initiated more stringent regulation of many powerful and addictive drugs, and in some cases outlawed them entirely.

A drug's legal status is not always indicative of how dangerous it is, however. Some drugs known to have harmful effects can be purchased legally in the United States and elsewhere. Nicotine, a key ingredient in cigarettes, is known to be highly addictive. In an effort to meet their bodies' demands for nicotine, smokers expose themselves to lung cancer, emphysema, and other life-threatening conditions. Despite these risks, nicotine is legal almost everywhere.

Other drugs that cannot be purchased or sold legally are the subject of much debate regarding their effects on physical and mental health. Marijuana, sometimes described as a gateway drug that leads users to other drugs, cannot legally be used, grown, or sold in this country. However, some research suggests that marijuana is neither addictive nor a gateway drug and that it might actually benefit cancer and AIDS patients by reducing pain and encouraging failing appetites. Despite these findings and occasional legislative attempts to change the drug's status, marijuana remains illegal.

The Drug Education Library examines the paradox of drugs and drug use in America by focusing on some of the most commonly used and abused drugs or categories of drugs available today. By discussing objectively the many types of drugs, their intended purposes, their effects (both planned and unplanned), and the controversies surrounding them, the books in this series provide readers with an understanding of the complex role drugs and drug use play in American society. Informative sidebars, annotated bibliographies, and organizations to contact lists highlight the text and provide young readers with many opportunities for further discussion and research.

![book icon] Introduction

The Cocaine Quagmire

Once considered a harmless source of pleasure and therapeutic benefit, today the drug cocaine is vilified as the cause of great misery and suffering for many who have succumbed to its euphoric effects. Yet, by nearly all acounts, cocaine is here to stay, despite the billions of dollars that government agencies around the world spend each year to eliminate it.

From the streets of cities as large as Los Angeles, New York, and Chicago, to small rural towns, Americans consume more cocaine than does any other citizenry in the world. An estimated 80 percent of all South American cocaine—approximately one thousand tons annually—finds its way to America's consumers. The size of the market for cocaine is staggering by any measure. An estimated 40 million Americans admit to having tried cocaine, either in powdered form or as crack. Moreover, between 2 and 4 million people admit to regular use of or addiction to cocaine. Faced with such numbers, American political and spiritual leaders have labeled cocaine use an epidemic.

Cocaine use swept across America during the 1970s, glamorized by rock stars, Hollywood personalities, and heroes of professional sports. Their widely publicized use of the drug brought it

Young men prepare crack cocaine for smoking. Cocaine use exploded in America's inner cities when this low-cost form of the drug became available in the 1980s.

to the attention of many Americans for the first time and gave it unprecedented status. More and more Americans began to explore the drug's euphoric effects, but cocaine's dark side began to emerge after a decade of use by people who first saw it as a fun and harmless drug. Addiction rates among young people and deaths from overdoses began to make headlines in newspapers and television news programs across the nation.

By the mid-1980s, what was already an epidemic was termed a crisis as a new, cheap form of cocaine called "crack" appeared on the streets. The low cost of crack made it the drug of choice among America's inner-city poor. Street gangs warred over the control of the sale and distribution of crack. This violence, on top of the crime committed by addicts to support their habits and hundreds of fatal overdoses annually, added to the misery and hopelessness of life in urban ghettos. This desperate situation became worse when hospitals began reporting an apparent increase in the number of babies born to crack-addicted mothers. These babies, who seem to share their mothers' addiction, were dubbed "crack babies" by the media.

A Costly Scourge

In addition to the human cost, the cocaine epidemic demands enormous amounts of money. Annually Americans are consuming roughly one thousand tons of cocaine at an estimated street cost of $90 billion—half of the value of all of America's agricultural products combined. On top of the amount of money spent purchasing cocaine, enormous sums of tax money are spent confiscating cocaine, prosecuting and incarcerating traffickers, and helping addicts to overcome their drug habits.

The Drug Enforcement Administration (DEA) spends $19 billion annually to stop illegal drugs from entering the country. Here, a Miami DEA agent guards 5,000 pounds of seized cocaine.

How much the cocaine and crack epidemic costs taxpayers is difficult to estimate because of the numbers of people involved, but some of that cost is clear enough. The U.S. government annually spends $2 billion in foreign aid to cocaine-producing countries to help them eliminate the drug at its source. In addition, the Drug Enforcement Administration (DEA) has an annual budget of $19 billion to intercept illegal drugs—cocaine among them—before they enter the country. Therapy for cocaine and crack addicts costs the taxpayers another $3 billion per year. On top of these known amounts are unknown sums spent by many branches of the military and local law enforcement agencies to intercept, arrest, prosecute, and incarcerate cocaine and crack traffickers and users.

Despite the costs, America's appetite for cocaine in its various forms seems insatiable. Political and civic leaders have organized to try to free America from the grip of the cocaine epidemic, but are divided on how best to do this. One faction proposes that America support a war on the coca fields in South America on the assumption that by destroying them, the supply of cocaine will dry up. Another faction proposes that America can stop cocaine trafficking only by providing more money for law enforcement, health practitioners, and social service workers to deal with the demand for the drug at home.

Neither of these two approaches has won the war on cocaine, however. Although use of cocaine in powder form has declined since 1985, crack use has increased. Both drugs, moreover, remain a major health and social problem and both continue to thrive on the streets of America regardless of the billions of dollars annually spent trying to stamp them out.

Chapter 1

Cocaine: A Once-Promising Drug

A t the beginning of the twentieth century, the medicine cabinets and pantries in many American homes held a variety of pills and foods containing cocaine as an ingredient. At the time, cocaine was considered to offer considerable benefits as an energy

An advertisement for cocaine toothache drops. In the early twentieth century, cocaine was thought of as a safe, effective energy booster and pain reliever.

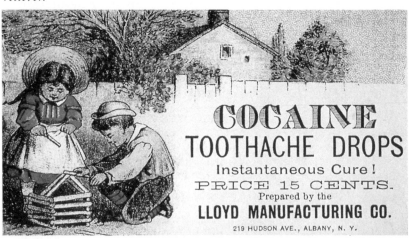

booster and as a topical remedy to relieve minor pain such as toothache. For example, in 1900, Sears, Roebuck, and Company advertised a product called Coca Wine. The advertisement for the wine boasted that it "sustains and refreshes both the body and brain. . . . It may be taken at any time with perfect safety . . . it has been effectually proven that in the same space of time more than double the amount of work could be undergone when Peruvian Wine of Coca was used, and positively no fatigue experienced."[1]

At the turn of the last century, both the medical profession and the pharmaceutical industry believed the claims that cocaine was useful and safe as an energy booster and for pain relief. Doses of the ingredient in foods and medicines were quite small, and most consumers did not experience problems from occasional use of such products. The few people who studied and wrote about cocaine during this era also believed that it had the potential to become a panacea—a wonder drug for the new century.

South American Origins

Although Americans in the early twentieth century saw cocaine as a modern miracle, Indian tribes living in the Andes ranges of South America had known about this drug for five thousand years. People living at high altitudes where the air is thin discovered that chewing the leaves of the indigenous coca plant increased their energy levels. This plant, known to modern-day botanists as *Erythroxylon coca,* not only boosted energy but seemed to impart a sense of well-being.

Unbeknownst to the Indians, the boost in energy they experienced came from a chemical agent in the leaves called cocaine alkaloid. This chemical also contributes to the coca plant's abundance—it acts as an insecticide, killing insects that try to feed on the plant.

Cocaine alkaloid occurs in low concentrations in the coca leaf, between .01 and .08 percent. As a result, chewing the leaves delivers a relatively low dose of the drug. At these low doses, people could partake of cocaine and still function normally. Furthermore, because the drug was never ingested in large quantities, its addictive qualities were less pronounced.

A Bolivian miner chews coca leaves. For five thousand years, South American Indian tribes have relieved physical discomforts by chewing coca leaves.

Indians noticed other beneficial effects besides the energy boost and euphoria. They discovered that chewing the coca leaf reduced the pain of tooth decay. They also found that chewing coca leaves relieved the physical discomfort that was part of long journeys on foot in the Andes. In fact, the use of coca was so common among mountain travelers that they measured the length of a journey by the number of wads of coca leaves chewed rather than by time or distance.

Introduction to Europe and America

The use of coca changed somewhat when the Spanish conquistadors first came to South America during the mid–sixteenth century. After the Spanish conquered the mountain tribes they forcibly converted them to Catholicism; Catholic priests, wishing to stamp out what they saw as a pagan practice, forbade the chewing of coca leaves. The Spanish, however, also forced the Indians to labor in the mines and fields and quickly observed that the workers tired more quickly when deprived of their coca leaves. To remedy this situation, the Spanish overseers distributed leaves to workers three to four times a day to increase their energy levels and productivity. The overseers began chewing the leaves as well and noted the same pleasant effects that the Indians experienced.

The Spanish sent shipments of the leaves back to Europe, where they became quite popular among the wealthy. The chewing of coca leaves did not, however, become widespread because shipping large quantities of leaves was not economically feasible and attempts to grow coca in Europe failed because the climate there was not suitable.

For nearly two hundred years, interest in coca leaves and their effect on the mind and body languished; for the most part the coca plant was merely a curiosity, of concern only to botanists such as Sir William Hooker, who in 1835 made the first accurate drawing of *Erythroxylon coca* for the magazine *Companion to the Botanical Magazine*. Cocaine's potential for medical use remained known to a few doctors, however, and in 1850 small amounts of diluted cocaine were used experimentally for the first time as an anesthetic during throat surgery. By 1855, scientists had accomplished a major breakthrough when they learned how to extract pure cocaine from the coca leaves in large volumes.

Although the medical community in Europe was just beginning to investigate the medical benefits of cocaine, soldiers had the most direct experience with the drug. Military leaders, learning of cocaine's effectiveness both as a painkiller and as an energy booster, tested cocaine

In 1835, botanist Sir William Hooker made the first accurate drawing of the coca plant.

on troops and found that these soldiers were able to endure longer marches and to fight more vigorously than soldiers who did not take the drug. Tests also indicated a distinct increase in soldiers' willingness to engage in fierce battles under the drug.

As the amount and availability of cocaine increased in Europe, some of it got into the hands of the public, which quickly discovered its ability to boost a person's energy level. Office workers found that cocaine seemed to make their day pass more swiftly, and athletes soon recognized that cocaine might have value in sports that required endurance. Several English long-distance runners, for example, attributed their success to chewing the coca leaves during races.

Medical Applications

Meanwhile, researchers continued to investigate the new drug's potential as a topical anesthetic. Doctors performing delicate operations on eyes discovered that cocaine numbed tissues, allowing them to perform surgery with only minor discomfort to the conscious patient, who could continue to move the eye as directed. The use of cocaine soon spread to surgery of other body parts, including the ears, nose, and mouth. Not only did cocaine numb the targeted area, but the patient remained awake. This allowed the doctors to converse with their patients during surgery, which helped the doctors to monitor their progress. Several pharmaceutical companies noted the success of cocaine as an anesthetic and during the 1880s began selling large amounts of the drug to hospitals.

Other physicians saw cocaine as possibly benefiting mental patients. In 1884, for example, the Austrian psychiatrist Sigmund Freud performed his own study of cocaine. Based on that study, Freud published a paper, *Über Coca,* in which he recommended the use of cocaine to treat a variety of conditions, including depression, morphine addiction, digestive disorders, and asthma. Freud tried taking cocaine himself and noted cocaine's effects as a mental stimulant and as an appetite depressant.

As cocaine became more commonly used, pharmaceutical companies perfected its manufacture and refinement. By the end of

Freud on Cocaine

In 1883 Austrian psychoanalyst Sigmund Freud read a study in a German medical journal about the beneficial effects of cocaine on German soldiers. He was fascinated by the elevating effects of the drug on soldiers' energy levels and decided to perform his own experiments, with himself as subject. At the website of BLTC Research, David Pierce reports that Freud wrote in his personal journal, "I take very small doses of it regularly and against depression and against indigestion, and with the most brilliant success." In 1884 Freud wrote *Über Coca*, in which he describes the effects from injection of cocaine in research animals as "the most gorgeous excitement."

When describing the effects of cocaine on humans in *Über Coca*, Freud reported that humans experience

> exhilaration and lasting euphoria, which in no way differs from the normal euphoria of the healthy person. . . . You perceive an increase of self-control and possess more vitality and capacity for work. . . . In other words, you are simply normal, and it is soon hard to believe you are under the influence of any drug. . . . Long intensive physical work is performed without any fatigue. . . . This result is enjoyed without any of the unpleasant after-effects that follow exhilaration brought about by alcohol. . . . Absolutely no craving for the further use of cocaine appears after the first, or even after repeated taking of, the drug.

the nineteenth century, companies were producing thousands of pounds of the drug each year. Cocaine, it appeared, was a drug with unlimited potential.

Commercial Value

Beneficial though cocaine seemed to the medical profession, its real growth was among people who were simply looking for an antidote to fatigue. Since no one in the medical profession had raised any serious reservations about possible harmful effects of cocaine, it appeared to be ideal as an energy booster. The earliest and most popular use of cocaine in a commercial product was the drink Vin Mariani, a mixture of wine and cocaine introduced in England in 1863. The beverage's popularity was widespread, perhaps due to the fact that Vin Mariani claimed it was endorsed by such luminaries as the American inventor Thomas Edison, British writer Sir Arthur Conan Doyle, England's Queen Victoria, and even the pope.

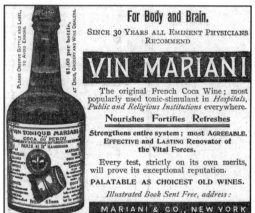

Vin Mariani, a drink made with wine and cocaine, was one of the first successful commercial products containing the drug.

Following the success of Vin Mariani, the Coca-Cola Company, in 1886, added 60 milligrams of cocaine to each bottle of its product and advertised it as a beverage that would invigorate the drinker. At about this same time, drug companies also saw the commercial value of cocaine and added it to products designed to relieve sore throats and toothaches.

By 1910 commercialization of products with cocaine was rampant as elixirs sold as magical potions guaranteed to make people happier and more energetic. Claims that these potions could cure everything from backaches to heart problems to difficulties in a person's love life caused congressional leaders to become alarmed at the widespread and uncontrolled use of cocaine in the nation's food and drugs.

The elevated moods and energy surges that cocaine induced in its users became widely known. Its effects on the body, however, remained a mystery. Although no ill effects had been observed, many doctors called for research to determine exactly what effects cocaine had on the body and whether any of these effects might have long-term adverse consequences.

Short-Term Physiological Effects

In the decades since research began, doctors have come to recognize that of the body's many systems, the cardiovascular system experiences the most noticeable short-term effects of cocaine use. The first of these is a rapid increase in the user's heart rate, which results in the heart pumping a greater volume of blood through the body. This is essentially the same effect that results from strenuous physical activity except that when cocaine is the cause, blood vessels narrow, forcing the heart to work not just faster but harder. Occasionally, cocaine also causes temporary rapid or erratic heart rhythms, increased blood pressure, and increased body temperature.

The central nervous system also experiences temporary physiological changes. As the cocaine carried by the bloodstream enters the brain, the electrical activity of the brain is temporarily altered as the cocaine is absorbed by cells called neurons. The absorption of cocaine alters the chemistry of the brain to increase production of the chemical dopamine. This change in brain chemistry is responsible for the sense of euphoria, sometimes referred to as a "rush" that is usually described in pleasurable terms as a sudden sense of excitement.

In most healthy people, most of these symptoms disappear within thirty to sixty minutes as the liver chemically decomposes

Dopamine Research

Although the neurotransmitter dopamine has been linked to the euphoric effects of cocaine for several years, recent research suggests that dopamine may only be part of the puzzle, and researchers now suspect that other neurotransmitters may also play a role.

In 1999 researchers at the University of North Carolina at Chapel Hill wrote a summary of dopamine research titled "Breakthrough? Study Finds Dopamine Cannot Be Source of Pleasure in Brain." University researchers implanted a tiny carbon fiber electrode in laboratory rats to stimulate the animals' brains' pleasure centers in the same way cocaine does. According to Dr. R. Mark Wightman, "We discovered that when we applied the electric shock to a pleasure sensor in the brain of untrained rats, we clearly saw dopamine, but when the animals themselves applied the shock, little or no dopamine appeared."

Wightman and his staff conclude that although dopamine may be involved in initial learning or anticipation of reward, it clearly is not responsible for continuous pleasure. Wightman suspects that cocaine stimulates production of other neurotransmitters such as serotonin, and that these may be responsible for continued pleasure.

the cocaine, which is then removed from the system by the kidneys.

Long-Term Physiological Effects

Researchers found little, if any, lingering effects from occasional use of cocaine. The long-term physiological effects for persistent cocaine use over many years are dramatic, however. Although the kidneys filter out cocaine after each use, the cumulative effect of hundreds of cocaine doses eventually alters the body's physiology and leads to physical damage. The organ that suffers the most damage is the brain. The more frequently cocaine users ingest the drug, the more frequently the blood vessels in the brain are narrowed and fail to adequately provide needed oxygen. Deprived of oxygen, brain cells die, so frequent cocaine use eventually compromises the brain's function. Furthermore, as the blood pressure in the millions of tiny constricted blood vessels and capillaries that supply the brain builds, they gradually break, causing hemorrhage. Dr. Thomas Kosten described this phenomenon during congressional testimony in 1999:

> If these vessels are blocked for even a few minutes, brain cells die and thinking, feeling, moving and life itself can cease. Cocaine blocks these blood vessels by constricting them and filling them with abnormal clotting cells called platelets. A large blockage like this leads to strokes in some cocaine abusers, and in most abusers the blockages are smaller, but occur in multiple places in the brain. These multiple blockages leave the cocaine abuser's brain shrunken, discolored and often poorly functioning.[2]

The restriction of blood supply to the brains of long-term cocaine users appears to be permanent. Scientists have recently been able to observe the restricted blood flow in the brains of such individuals. Using an imaging technique called positron emission tomography (PET), scientists can document the flow of blood in the brain tissue. When the researchers compared PET scans of long-term cocaine abusers with PET scans of normal non–cocaine abusers, they found that the abusers had less blood flow in several areas of the brain. When the researchers performed PET scans again ten days after cocaine use had been discontinued, the blood flow deficits remained even though the subjects in the study had stopped using cocaine.

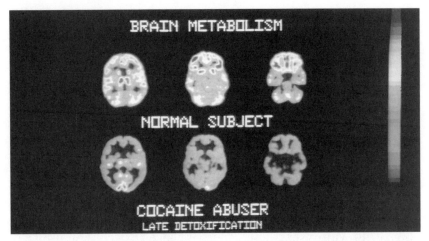

PET scans compare the brain of a normal subject (top) to that of a cocaine abuser (bottom). Such scans have revealed that cocaine abusers have less blood flow in several areas of the brain than nonusers.

Not only does the cocaine-related brain damage appear permanent, but the constricted arteries are vulnerable to strokes, which in turn can cause paralysis of parts of the body, the complete loss of speech, loss of memory, and even death. The overall effect is similar to greatly accelerating the aging process. Dr. R. I. Herning, a researcher working on the effects of long-term cocaine use, says, "Our data suggest that cocaine abusers in their thirties have arteries that are as constricted as those of normal subjects in their sixties." [3]

The cardiovascular system can also suffer damage from long-term cocaine use. The heart, in response to blood vessel constrictions, pumps faster and with greater force in order to meet the oxygen requirements of the body. When the heart is forced to sustain these elevated rates and pressures, it is vulnerable to serious, even deadly problems. For example, the heart can begin to beat erratically, which is called ventricular fibrillation. During an attack of fibrillation, little blood is pumped and without immediate treatment, the victim can die. The heart can also race at rates three to four times normal, a condition called tachycardia. Persistent tachycardia can lead to death.

Medical researchers have proven that long-term cocaine use can cause permanent and massive damage to the brain and heart. Understanding the physical damage inflicted on the body by cocaine, however, has been far easier for researchers than understanding the psychological effects of cocaine. Central to this understanding is the question of whether cocaine is addictive or not.

Is Cocaine Addictive?

The debate over whether or not cocaine is addictive is ongoing and complicated. The majority of mental health professionals take the view that regular cocaine users cannot voluntarily stop taking the drug. In this sense, cocaine meets the definition of an addictive drug. Moreover, these experts believe that cocaine use leads to physical changes in the brain that encourage continued use. Journalist Norbert R. Myslinski reports:

> According to Prof. Karen Bolla of Johns Hopkins University, cocaine impairs memory, manual dexterity, and decision making for at least a month. Her study suggests damage to the brain's prefrontal cortex, leading to loss of control over consumption of the drug. A deadly spiral is set up, making it more and more difficult for the addict to quit. Continued drug abuse becomes increasingly a matter of brain damage and less a matter of weak character.[4]

Another study performed by researchers at Rockefeller University in New York City confirms Bolla's conclusions and provides a detailed explanation of the brain chemistry of a chronic cocaine user. The Rockefeller University investigators found that repeated exposure to cocaine causes a change at the molecular level that alters a brain protein called cyclin-dependent kinase 5. The researchers believe that altering this protein leads to cocaine addiction. Dr. Alan I. Leshner, director of the National Institute on Drug Abuse (NIDA), says, "This research provides a valuable insight into the step-by-step molecular adaptations that the brain makes in response to drugs. These adaptations result in long-term changes at the cellular level that are involved in the development of addiction."[5]

The medical view that cocaine is addictive is generally shared by long-term cocaine users themselves. One self-confessed addict, when asked how cocaine use—particularly in the form known as crack— could be stopped, says, "You can't . . . period. It will be on this earth as long as there is people. As long as there is people, there will be people smoking crack cocaine." When asked what he would say to anyone thinking about trying cocaine, he says, "Don't ever do it, don't even try it once. You do it once, I don't [care] who you are, you will be hooked for the rest of your life."[6] The urge to keep using the drug is strong enough to motivate some addicts to resort to extreme measures. Gilda Berger quotes a crack user in her book *Crack: The New Drug Epidemic,* who claims, "I'd kill for it!"[7]

Cocaine Comparisons

Commonly used addictive drugs have many different characteristics. The following table, provided by Dr. Jack E. Henningfield in the *New York Times* article "Is Nicotine Addictive? It Depends on Whose Criteria You Use," compares cocaine with five other drugs and ranks them according to five addictive characteristics. A rank of 1 indicates least effect; a rank of 6 indicates highest potency.

Dependence: How difficult it is for the user to quit; the relapse rate; the percentage of people who eventually become dependent; the rating users give their own need for the substance; and the degree to which the substance will be used in the face of evidence that it causes harm.

Withdrawal: Presence and severity of characteristic withdrawal symptoms.

Tolerance: How much of the substance is needed to satisfy increasing cravings for it, and the level of stable need that is eventually reached.

Reinforcement: A measure of the substance's ability, in human and animal tests, to get users to take it again and again, and in preference to other substances.

Intoxication: Though not usually counted as a measure of addiction in itself, the level of intoxication is associated with addiction and increases the personal and social damage a substance may do.

Drug	Dependence	Withdrawal	Tolerance	Reinforcement	Intoxication
Nicotine	6	4	5	3	2
Heroin	5	5	6	5	5
Cocaine	4	3	3	6	4
Alcohol	3	6	4	4	6
Caffeine	2	2	2	1	1
Marijuana	1	1	1	2	3

An addict smokes from a crack pipe.

Powerful as the evidence is that cocaine is addictive, some medical researchers disagree over just *how* addictive the drug is. One of the most compelling arguments against strong addictive properties is the fact that a relatively small percentage of people who use cocaine actually become addicted. Various national agencies report an average cocaine addiction rate of about 1 percent of individuals who have tried the drug—lower than the addiction rate for nicotine among those who have tried tobacco. If cocaine is so addictive, they argue, why is the addiction rate so low?

As the debate over its addictive potential continues, the reality of nearly epidemic cocaine use in America remains, despite the fact that the drug is illegal in every state.

Chapter 2

Illicit Use of Cocaine

The spread of cocaine use among Americans during the early twentieth century began to attract the attention of the medical community and national leaders. Government officials decided to investigate the use of cocaine and learned that large numbers of citizens were buying cocaine not in the form of additives to foods, beverages, and medicines intended to treat specific medical conditions, but in its pure form for the pleasurable sensation the drug induced. Evidence that cocaine consumption might have slipped beyond the bounds of medical use caused alarm.

Declared Illegal

As cocaine use rose, hospitals began reporting an alarming increase of illness linked to the drug. In 1912, for example, five thousand deaths were directly or indirectly attributed to cocaine. In 1914 the U.S. government responded by declaring cocaine a controlled substance, making its use illegal except when prescribed by a doctor. As a result, cocaine use dropped dramatically and imports of coca leaves, which in 1914 had been estimated at about 450 tons, fell by two-thirds. Consumption of cocaine continued to decline through the 1930s and 1940s, in part because

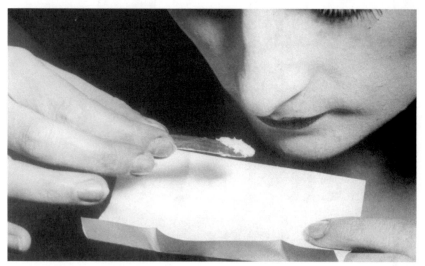

A woman snorts cocaine in 1935. After rising in the early 1900s, cocaine use declined in the 1930s and 1940s.

discretionary income fell sharply during the Great Depression and in part because many men who might have had the opportunity and money to use the drug were fighting World War II. This trend of declining use, however, would not continue indefinitely.

Cocaine During the 1970s

After more than two decades of relative obscurity, cocaine re-emerged on the American drug scene in the early 1970s. Deterred by the obvious addictiveness and social stigma of drugs like heroin and the occasional "bad trip" associated with hallucinogens such as LSD, some Americans saw cocaine as a relatively harmless "recreational" drug. Its potential for harm was downplayed, especially since markedly successful individuals in the entertainment industry seemed to use the drug with impunity. As movie stars, rock musicians, and sports heroes openly admitted using cocaine and enjoying its euphoric effects, its popularity and image soared among the general population.

Cocaine quickly occupied a niche in American popular culture. The rock song "Cocaine," recorded by Eric Clapton, Richie Havens, Dave Van Ronk, the Jack Saints, and DRG Compilations, bolstered the drug's cool image. More songs with "cocaine" in the title followed, performed by some of America's most popular singers. Dozens of movies appeared featuring scences that both destigmatized and satirized the use of the drug, depicting cocaine users as fun, successful people. A scene in Woody Allen's film *Annie Hall*, for example, depicts guests at a party comically sneezing after inhaling the powder. The Albert Brooks film *Lost in America* includes a scene featuring people laughing with white powder on the tips of their noses. According to a study led by Donald F. Roberts, Thomas More Storke Professor of Communication at Stanford University, who researched the movie industry's pleasurable portrayal of drugs, "Of the movies showing drugs, marijuana appeared most frequently (51 percent), followed by powder cocaine (33 percent)."[8]

Cocaine use among professional athletes was even more common than among musicians or actors. Many athletes believed that cocaine acted as a stimulant that sustained their energy level, allowed them to endure greater pain, and speeded their reaction time on the field. The consequences of cocaine use seemed minor: At the time, even though the drug was illegal, professional sports organizations did not specifically ban the use of cocaine. And law enforcement authorities tended to be reluctant to arrest high-profile players for local basketball and football teams.

The more that sports and popular culture icons glorified cocaine the more the public wanted to experience the same exhilaration, despite a rise in price to over $100 per gram. As more and more Americans tried cocaine, doubts about its alleged harmlessness once again began to grow in the minds of many health professionals. Deaths attributed to cocaine were routinely reported by the press,

Cocaine use soared in the 1970s, popularized by rock stars like Eric Clapton (right) who recorded the hit song "Cocaine."

although they were dismissed by cocaine users as freak accidents or as examples of the consequences of reckless abuse.

Cocaine's Changing Image in the 1980s

Despite growing concerns about its possible dangers, cocaine use in America grew through the early 1980s. In 1985, estimates by various government health agencies placed the number of people who had used it at least once at about 7 million. Of this number, about 5.5 million used it occasionally; about 600,000 were considered habitual users, defined by using it more than 51 times a year.

During this period, evidence pointing to the health risks of cocaine use continued to surface. Stories of death due to cocaine overdoses on college campuses and in affluent neighborhoods began replacing the glittery talk of recreational use by sports and movie stars. For example, the death of college basketball star Len Bias from a cocaine overdose received front-page coverage. Not only were overdoses becoming recognized as a problem, but gradually people began to recognize that once the initial euphoria wore off, cocaine had the insidious quality of inducing a state of depression that triggered a craving for more. Just as ominously, the medical professions began to recognize that many recreational users were showing signs of the ill effects of heavy use.

As it became clear that more and more people were regularly using cocaine, medical researchers began to study the drug's psychological as well as physiological effects. What these scientists discovered was unsettling.

Cocaine-related deaths, like that of college basketball star Len Bias in 1986, brought increased attention to the risks of cocaine use.

Short-Term Psychological Effects

The immediate psychological effect of cocaine ingestion is euphoria. The intensity of this effect depends on how fast the drug reaches the brain; that is, the faster cocaine reaches the brain, the more intense the euphoria. For the first few minutes after inhaling powdered cocaine, or the first few seconds after injecting it, the user experiences the onset of the euphoria, known as a rush. Users describe such feelings as a heightened state of pleasure, a profound sense of mastery over their personal affairs, a sense of cleverness, and an unquestioned confidence in their ability to achieve their goals. Many users claim that the drug helps them perform many physical and intellectual tasks more quickly. As one youth describes it, cocaine made him feel "as if I was going up in a flying machine" or "as if I was a millionaire and could do anything I pleased."[9] In addition to the sense of euphoria, many users describe being more energetic, talkative, and more acutely aware of the sensations of sound, taste, color, and touch. Officer Gordon James Knowles of the Pearl Harbor Police Narcotics Division questioned a cocaine user and dealer named Carl, whose description of the initial rush also explains its value as an escape from reality:

> I feel high like you wouldn't believe. . . . It's hard to explain how you feel. . . . I feel like I'm floating on air. . . . On one hand . . . I feel like an idiot for doing what I'm doing and that is absolutely nothing except getting high, but on the other hand, I love it because I'm getting high as much as I want, when I want . . . and that makes up for everything else. You see people who live on the streets, 99 percent of them snort coke because it's a way for them to forget about life . . . forget about the things you wanted in life . . . this is like a replacement.[10]

New pharmacological research supports a widely held theory that cocaine-induced euphoria is tied to a chemical messenger in the brain called dopamine.

Dopamine is a special chemical, called a neurotransmitter, that has the job of transmitting electrical messages from one nerve cell, or neuron, to the next. Researchers, who have identified more than fifty different neurotransmitters, believe that dopamine is the one responsible for interacting, or binding, with the psychoactive chemicals found in cocaine. Dopamine is called the "pleasure neurotransmitter" because the impulses it transmits impart a pleasurable sensation.

Dopamine flows from neurons into the synapses, the tiny spaces between neurons, to form a temporary bridge that carries the signal across the synapse. Normally, after a neuron has transmitted its signal to the next neuron, the dopamine leaves these spaces, returning to the same neuron that released it in a recycling process called re-uptake.

If cocaine is present in the brain while an electrical signal is taking place, scientists believe it blocks the re-uptake process, resulting in a buildup of dopamine in the synapses which creates an abnormally acute sense of pleasure. As the buildup of the dopamine neurotransmitter continues, it causes the euphoria commonly reported as the pleasurable rush.

Exactly why this pleasurable sensation occurs is still largely a mystery. However, Dr. Donald W. Landry, associate professor of

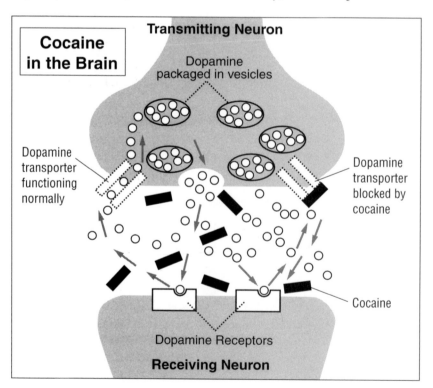

medicine at Columbia University, speculates that the answer lies in the limbocortical region deep in the center of the brain. Cocaine, he suspects,

> stimulates a neural "reward pathway" that evolved in the ancestors of mammals more than 100 million years ago. This pathway activates the so-called limbocortical region of the brain, which controls the most basic emotions and behaviors . . . [that] undoubtedly conferred a survival advantage. The same structures persist today and provide a physiological basis for our subjective perception of pleasure. When natural brain chemicals known as neurotransmitters stimulate these circuits, a person feels "good."[11]

When all the cocaine has reacted however, the re-uptake process begins and the dopamine levels drop, causing the euphoria to disappear as fast as it first appeared. The absence of euphoria is experienced as depression. The user also experiences irritability, fatigue, and an intense craving for more of the drug to escape the depression.

It is worth noting that this view of how dopamine causes its pleasurable effects is still theoretical, as Dr. Solomon Snyder of Johns Hopkins University indicates: "Again, *we do not know for certain* exactly how the brain regulates specific behaviors, but we can formulate some educated guesses and . . . we can use these guesses as the basis for the next important advances in understanding."[12]

For those who have experienced the cocaine cycle of "rush-to-crash" many times, the psychological effects have long-term consequences that become a constant part of the habitual user's life.

Long-Term Psychological Effects

Long-term cocaine use causes clearly visible psychological changes in users. Although doctors cannot say conclusively how long-term cocaine use affects the chemistry of the brain, subtle changes take place that constitute what clinicians call cocaine psychosis. Those who experience cocaine psychosis lose contact with reality and the ability to function normally. The most common manifestations of cocaine psychosis are hallucinations, paranoia, depression, and anxiety.

A crack addict lights up, her body ravaged from heavy drug use.

The user who suffers from cocaine psychosis may experience hallucinations that are highly animated and dramatic sensory distortions, such as seeing objects suddenly change form. One of the most common hallucinations among long-term cocaine users is the sense that insects are crawling on their bodies. So distinctive is this hallucination that the imagined insects are known as "coke bugs." Other hallucinations may take the form of hearing people laughing and talking when no one else is in the room, or smelling the aroma of food when none is present.

In addition to hallucinations, addicts may experience periods of paranoia; that is, they may think that people with hostile or harmful intentions are plotting against them. The most common example of paranoid thinking among cocaine users is falsely believing that the police are tapping their telephones.

Depression, a dulled mood and loss of energy and enthusiasm for normal activities, also often accompanies the paranoia and hallucinations. Excessive cocaine use commonly leads to a disinterest in friends, school, or usual family activities. Adding to the misery of a cocaine psychosis sufferer is the anxiety that goes with constant uncertainty over finding the next fix of cocaine.

Antisocial Behavior

Although not all long-term cocaine users experience cocaine psychosis, those who do are unable to function in society. Thus, cocaine psychosis is likely to affect those personally and professionally connected to the user as well as the user himself.

Those suffering from cocaine psychosis display a variety of antisocial behaviors, such as deception, violence, and isolation.

This deception often begins with lying to friends and family about the cost and frequency of cocaine use; experts in addictive behavior note that self-deception in the form of blaming others for the user's addiction is also common. If this pattern continues unchecked, many regular cocaine users escalate their deception to nonviolent forms of criminal behavior such as shoplifting, burglary, and forgery to pay for their cocaine habits.

If nonviolent criminal behavior fails to generate enough money to meet the addict's cocaine needs, violence is often the next step. Violent behavior can range from verbal assaults to the extremes of physical assault, murder, and suicide. Such antisocial behavior often results from inability to resolve their distress through conflict resolution techniques such as negotiation and compromise. The association between prolonged use of cocaine and violent behavior is well documented. One criminologist, James Lardner, held

Coke Bugs

One of the most common manifestations of cocaine psychosis is a sensory hallucination experienced by many long-term users who feel bugs crawling all over their bodies and in their mouths. This hallucination is so common that it has become known as "coke bugs." Eugene Richards, in his book *Cocaine True, Cocaine Blue,* interviews a cocaine addict who tells this story about coke bugs:

> I knew this guy, every time he got high, he thought he felt these little bugs, and he would pick at his skin and bleed. He had holes all over, he'd swear he'd see them moving, try to get them with clippers and scissors and razors. Try to dig them out. Finally, he just got a thing of Black Flag, the roach spray, and sprayed his whole body, and wound up dying. But cocaine is not supposed to do that. It does that when you do too much.

conversations with inmates in New York's Rikers Island prison and reported that

> interviews with criminals, accused criminals, former criminals, and street-savvy kids in Phoenix, New York City, and Newark, N.J., highlighted another important development: a new awareness of the harm done by hard drugs, and especially by cocaine and crack cocaine, associated with some of the worst violence of the past decade.[13]

A man buys crack cocaine from a dealer. Cocaine addiction can be very costly, and some addicts resort to criminal behavior to pay for their habits.

Cocaine and Crime

Many cocaine and crack addicts support their habits through criminal activities. Eugene Richards, author of *Cocaine True, Cocaine Blue,* interviews Sally, a teenage cocaine addict with an already long history of crime:

> I got shot selling drugs. . . . The guy pulled up a .22 from the side of the car. That was years ago because I'm sixteen this year. I just got out [of jail] in January, armed theft and robbery. But I had no gun. I had some money and a lady's pocket book and then I got caught in a stolen car. Now I live with my parents, though my favorite thing is still going downtown with other girls. I hop on the trolley downtown to see if I can steal something. Easiest stuff is pants, silk shirt, socks. I go in there and try on the pants and put my jeans on top of it, then walk out the door. Sometimes I take leather pants and get thirty, forty dollars back up here.
>
> My mom's around here somewhere. I don't really do tricks [prostitution], but sometimes I sell drugs, making four hundred to five hundred dollars a week. If you add it all up, though, I blow a lot of it smoking turbos [crack mixed with marijuana] and drinking beer.

Often, however, it is the addict who is the victim of the violence. The National Institute on Drug Abuse (NIDA), for example, reports:

> Dr. Kenneth Tardiff of Cornell University Medical College in New York City headed a team of researchers that studied the 4,298 homicides that occurred in New York City during 1990 and 1991. Cocaine was found in the bodies of 31 percent of the victims. Homicide victims may have provoked violence through irritability, paranoid thinking, or verbal or physical aggression, which are known to be pharmacological effects of cocaine.[14]

The deceptions and antisocial behavior that the cocaine abuser inevitably relies on to support his or her habit frequently alienate both friends and family. The resulting isolation tends to reinforce the user's paranoia and depression, creating a vicious cycle that is destructive not just for the addict but for all those who deal with him or her.

Chapter 3

The Crack Epidemic

A s extreme as some cocaine-induced behaviors can be, they are relatively mild when compared with the behavior induced by crack, a derivative of cocaine. In 1985, when the price of cocaine had soared to $150 a gram, plastic vials containing what looked like tiny soap chips began selling on the streets of low-income

A small amount of pure cocaine is combined with water and either ammonia or sodium bicarbonate. The mixture is then dried, forming rocks of crack.

neighborhoods for $5 to $10 a "rock." Crack cocaine had arrived on America's streets and, unlike pricey cocaine, just about anyone who wanted crack could afford it.

The active ingredient of crack is cocaine. Working in illicit "kitchens," individuals manufacture crack by adding ammonia or sodium bicarbonate and water to pure cocaine, drying the mixture, and then crumbling the residue into small rocks. Adulterated this way, a gram of cocaine makes enough crack to satisfy many users.

Though it is made from a relatively small amount of powdered cocaine, crack is extremely potent. Because crack is smoked, the active chemicals reach the brain in seconds compared to the ten to fifteen minutes powdered cocaine requires. Crack's almost instantaneous delivery to the brain provides a more highly concentrated impact than does snorted cocaine, which loses potency as it travels through the bloodstream.

Suddenly, cocaine was no longer just for the well-to-do. Dealers sold crack in packets of two to five rocks, meaning that even someone earning the minimum wage could afford to get high.

The synthesizing of crack from cocaine boosted the sale of both forms of the drug and dramatically increased the number of users. Crack dealers quickly moved their operations into low-income neighborhoods. Just as cocaine had been labeled the drug of the wealthy, crack was labeled the drug of choice of the inner city or ghetto.

With the availability of this potent, inexpensive form of cocaine, millions of low-income workers and adolescents began trying the drug. What they quickly—and unexpectedly—learned was that the intensity of the crack rush brought with it greater risk of addiction than did cocaine. By the end of the 1980s, crack use and the problems it caused reached epidemic levels.

As the use of crack spread, epidemiologists recognized that crack was rapidly becoming a serious threat primarily to the poor who lacked the educational and financial resources to cope with the destructive effects of the drug. Not only were the nation's poor ill-equipped to deal with crack's effects, but the very attributes that made crack affordable to the poor guaranteed that it

Crack use has become an epidemic in inner-city neighborhoods, where low cost and high potency make the drug attractive and affordable.

would exacerbate other problems that already made life in the nation's inner cities a daily struggle.

Cocaine Versus Crack

Although crack is derived from cocaine and is classified by federal and state law enforcement agencies as a form of cocaine, each form of the drug works differently in the body. Unlike cocaine, crack affects the user within seconds; similarly, its effects wear off more quickly, lasting only between five and ten minutes. Unfortunately for crack users, the intense rush is so pleasurable that users want more as soon as the effects wear off, and addiction is more likely. Moreover, since the euphoria wears off much faster than it does with cocaine, users must smoke many times a day to keep the inevitable depression at bay. Drug researcher Elisabeth Ryan describes the differences between inhaling powdered cocaine and smoking crack this way:

It may take several minutes to feel the effects of snorting coke, and the "high" lasts for about 20 minutes to a half hour. Crack, on the other hand, is felt within a few seconds, and the short but very intense high lasts only for five or ten minutes, followed by a very intense crash. Cocaine is psychologically and physically addictive to many people, but it usually takes from two to five years for the addiction to develop. Crack, because it operates so quickly, is also very quickly addictive. Almost without exception, users become addicted within the first few uses, sometimes from the very first use.[15]

The Inner-City Dilemma

The destructive potential of crack was soon apparent. During the late 1980s and early 1990s, hospital emergency rooms began reporting hundreds of crack-related deaths and secondary illness associated with crack addiction. Social services were swamped by children abandoned by their crack-addicted parents. Local police and federal drug enforcement officers packed local jails with inner-city crack users and dealers in an attempt to stem the spread of the drug and the crimes that went with it.

Most visible to Americans was televised coverage of the violence that accompanied the crack epidemic. Local street gangs recognized that they could make money by selling crack. To eliminate competition, gangs fought for control of crack trafficking and as a result neighborhoods began to resemble shooting ranges. Handguns became the standard weapons for enforcing control of trafficking in neighborhoods. High school and even junior high school students began dealing crack and carrying guns to school campuses. Gun battles among crack dealers, along with the frequent confrontations between the crack community and the police, created an unprecedented atmosphere of violence in many inner-city neighborhoods.

Crack houses soon appeared in East Coast slums as dealers and users found places to carry on their activities out of view of both the police and rival gangs. Although crack houses gave dealers and their customers the protection they sought, these structures contributed to an image of decay in America's inner cities. Often lacking running water, electricity, or trash collection, crack houses were breeding grounds for disease. An addict who overdosed

Police officers survey the debris inside a filthy crack house in Washington, D.C.

there was unlikely to receive help because no one else was responsible enough to summon police or medics for assistance.

In an attempt to maintain order for the majority of lawful citizens in the inner cities, some police departments adopted the strategy of arresting as many crack users and dealers as possible. When police identified crack houses, they arrested anyone they found there. Gang members known to traffic in crack were rounded up in mass arrests.

Focusing enforcement on crack houses and their occupants succeeded in eliminating some crack houses, but what the nation began to see was jails filled with disproportionately large numbers of African American and Hispanic youths. To the complexities of the crack epidemic was added the perception that the war on crack was actually racially motivated. Minority leaders in many communities complained that the police were intentionally targeting the small-time minority users and dealers while turning a blind eye toward the big-time traffickers, who were often white. Some community leaders who raised allegations of racism demanded investigations into police policies.

Crack Houses

One widely known outgrowth of crack use is the so-called crack house, where crack addicts congregate to buy and smoke crack or inject cocaine. Mariella, a longtime cocaine addict, describes the scene inside a crack house she frequents to Eugene Richards in *Cocaine True, Cocaine Blue.*

> They [cocaine users] get sick in there if they live in there. You see them laying around. They need water to mix up the drugs, the dope or the coke, and the crack, so especially if they're homeless or hookers, they'll get water from anywhere.
>
> Yeah, I think it's four bucks to shoot up. Other places are like a buck or two, just a dollar or two to get in, and you just gotta do your shit and get out. Yeah, it's usually an abandoned building, but they take their squatters' rights or whatever the hell you want to call it. You're taking a big chance going in there, because you get ripped off, you get mugged. You can die.

A police officer raids a crack house in an abandoned factory in Bridgeport, Connecticut.

Police departments accused of intentionally targeting minorities for arrest generally denied the charges. Law enforcement per-
sonnel argued that they were arresting more people of color for
crack violations precisely because crack was more commonly used
among minorities than among whites. To support this view, police cited studies such as the National Household Survey on Drug
Abuse (NHSDA), which found in 1997 that Hispanics were 30
percent more likely than whites to use crack and that blacks were
133 percent more likely than whites to use crack.

Statistics such as the NHSDA study did little to quell accusa-
tions of racism. Many leaders in the black community sought
greater leniency on the part of the police toward minority users
while suggesting that arresting the crack kingpins would be a
more effective way of curtailing the crack epidemic. These leaders
further suggested that money spent on arresting users could be
better spent preventing the drugs from reaching minority communities in the first place.

Regardless of the politics of how police departments handled
the crack epidemic, health professionals, public school adminis-

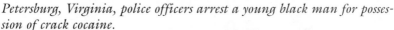

*Petersburg, Virginia, police officers arrest a young black man for posses-
sion of crack cocaine.*

trators, and social service providers quickly recognized that a crack culture was evolving in America's inner cities, creating a complex web of interrelated crime and suffering.

Crack-Related Crime

As the use of crack spread, crime followed closely behind. According to statistics compiled by large metropolitan police departments, the sale and use of crack spawns far more crime than the sale and use of most other drugs. Statistics also indicate that crack is responsible for an increase in the violence of crimes committed. The U.S. Sentencing Commission held a hearing on cocaine and crack in which criminologist Dr. Steven Belenko addressed the commission as an expert witness. According to the commission's published report, "Dr. Steven Belenko stated that he had analyzed arrest data for crack cocaine sellers and determined that, relative to powder cocaine sellers, crack cocaine sellers had higher arrest rates for both nondrug and violent crimes."[16]

Crime associated with America's underground crack industry is a large, violent, and complex problem. In addition to possession and sale of crack, which are violations of the law, crack dealers and users perpetrate many other crimes as well. Not only do innocent people become victims, people within the crack culture are themselves victimized.

Because they need many doses of the drug to feed their habit, addicts can easily spend over $100 a day to satisfy their craving for crack. Handicapped by the effects of the drug, most addicts are incapable of maintaining full-time legitimate jobs to earn this much money, much less pay for their other daily needs. For many of these people, the only option is to turn to crime: selling crack themselves, armed robbery, mugging, shoplifting, auto theft, and prostitution. Ironically, although hundreds of millions of dollars' worth of goods are stolen each year to support crack habits, more often than not, dealers and users victimize each other.

Within the complex network of drug distribution, dealers and users commit many crimes against each other. Traffickers fight over control of sales in particular neighborhoods, dealers rob rival dealers of drugs and money, and dealers sell diluted crack to their customers. From time to time, gang members who have become police informants are exposed; they are often killed in retaliation. Hierarchies within drug gangs are established and maintained with force, and dozens of minor rules within the crack "community" are violently enforced. Controlling street dealers, for example, is generally done through physical threats. Belenko states that the need to maintain control over street dealers creates an atmosphere where everyone is likely to "use . . . violence to maintain discipline, resolve disputes, and enforce control." [17] These types of crime are a part of the crack business and, because that business is illegal, most victims are unwilling to turn to the police and cannot ask courts to redress their grievances. As one expert notes, "In an underground economy, you can't sue. So you use violence to enforce your breaches of contract or perceived breaches of contract." [18]

Youth and the Web of Crime

Neighborhood youths are often more likely to be drawn into the web of crack-related crime than are older residents. Criminologists have found that those who control the crack trade intentionally recruit teenagers as young as thirteen who have criminal records to serve as street dealers because they tend to be easily intimidated and are often more willing to commit crimes than teens without criminal backgrounds.

The correlation between crack and crime against other members of society is well documented. Whenever police arrest people for serious crimes, suspects are tested for the presence of illegal drugs in their systems. In 1999, the Drug Enforcement Administration (DEA) compiled statistics on the results of drug tests on men arrested in major cities. They found an alarmingly high proportion—39.9 percent of suspects—tested positive, suggesting that many crimes are committed in order to support drug habits.

The increased level of violence among criminals due to crack changed entire neighborhoods. As crack-related violence rose, law-abiding citizens, fearing for their lives, converted their homes

St. Louis police officers remove police tape near where a fellow officer was shot and killed by a man in possession of crack cocaine.

and apartments into fortresses. They bolted steel bars over street-level windows and many bought handguns for self-protection. Even though most of these neighborhoods already had a history of crime, few had experienced such a high level of violent crime in the past.

Mandatory Minimum Sentencing

Local police forces, realizing that they were losing the war on crack, turned to the federal government for help. In an attempt to help police regain control of inner-city streets and protect innocent citizens from the destructive tendencies of the crack culture, Congress passed new laws aimed at removing crack dealers from society.

In 1986 Congress established mandatory minimum sentences for convicted dealers, responding to public outcry that judges sentencing cocaine and crack offenders were too lenient. Lawmakers made a distinction between powdered cocaine and crack: The mandatory minimum sentence for possession of five hundred grams of powdered cocaine was five years in prison. The same sentence was mandated for possession of just five grams of crack.

Although the stated objective of these mandatory minimum sentences was to reduce the amount of cocaine and crack available on the street, the laws generated a great deal of controversy. First, many community leaders question whether harsher sentences for crack offenses have actually reduced the volume of crack. According to the NHSDA, there are about six hundred thousand regular crack users in the United States and this number has remained stable for the past ten years. Some believe that the stabilized rate is evidence that mandatory minimum sentencing has been successful. On the other hand, those who believe that the minimum standards have not been successful argue that the number of crack users should have dropped rather than remained stable.

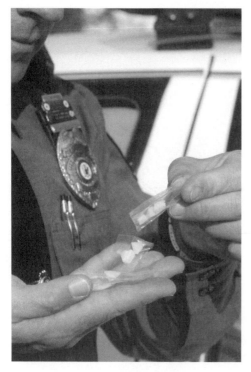

In 1986, Congress passed a law which created a mandatory minimum sentence of five years in prison for possession of just five grams of crack.

Second, some charged racism was a factor in leveling harsher sentences on offenders locked up for crack possession, who were predominantly black or Hispanic, than on cocaine offenders, who were more often white. According to David T. Courtwright, professor of history and health sciences at the University of North Florida, "The result was that, by 1993, federal prison sentences for blacks averaged 41 percent longer than those of whites, with the crack/powder distinction being the major reason for the difference."[19]

Opponents of mandatory minimum sentences argue that the laws are racist because the fact that most crack dealers and users are minorities means that the harsher mandatory minimum sentences affect minorities disproportionately. Journalist Jann Wenner, founder of *Rolling Stone* magazine, summarized the sense of racism in the sentencing disparity in the following observation:

> I certainly think they [the laws] should be reexamined—and the disparities are unconscionable between crack and powdered cocaine. . . . The Republican Congress was willing to narrow, but not eliminate, them on the theory that people who use crack are more violent than people who use cocaine. Well, what they really meant was that people who use crack are more likely to be poor and, coincidentally, black or brown and, therefore, not have money. Whereas, people who use cocaine were more likely to be rich, pay for it, and therefore be peaceable.[20]

Supporters of minimum sentences counter the racism allegation by pointing out that crack is a factor in more violent crimes than cocaine is. Moreover, supporters contend, minority residents are often the ones who summon the police to make arrests and to close down crack houses.

Although opinions differ on the value of mandatory minimum sentencing in controlling the crack epidemic, there appears to be universal agreement that something has to be done to intervene in the destruction of families caused by crack use.

Dysfunctional Families

One of the tragedies of crack use is the harm it inflicts on innocent family members. Individuals trapped within crack dependency are typically incapable of normal functioning and their

families tend to suffer from confusion, unpredictability, and violence. Care and concern for children is often overlooked by crack-
addicted parents in the never-ending pursuit of the next fix. Some
parents even expect their children to deal crack to help shore up
their sagging finances. Jonathan Beaty, a journalist researching
the dysfunctional effects of crack on families, reports:

> The extra cash that appears on the kitchen table can persuade parents to
> look the other way while their children are heading into trouble. Denise
> Robinson, founder of the Detroit community-action group Saving Our
> Kids, even recalls a mother who dissuaded her son from returning to
> school. "He had been a good student. He had good grades," says Robin-
> son. "But he was making $600 a week dealing crack. So his mother
> wanted him to keep dealing." [21]

Poverty is one of the most common causes of family dysfunction,
and crack use only deepens family poverty. When most of a family's
financial resources are spent on crack, little is left over for basic family
needs. Not only does crack use up most of a family's money, few
crack addicts are capable of full-time regular employment because of
their need to smoke crack several times a day. According to Gilda

---

*Crack addicts, consumed by their need to smoke crack several times a day,
are rarely able to hold down a job or fulfill parental responsibilities.*

Berger in *Crack: The New Drug Epidemic,* "Experts have found that while cocaine addicts manage to maintain their jobs, it is almost impossible for crack addicts to keep up their normal lives."[22]

In addition to financial strains, an addicted parent is unable to fulfill other basic responsibilities. Promises to children are neither kept nor remembered, and parents' expectations of children vary from one day to the next. Parents may be strict at times, indifferent at others, or absent from the home for days at a time. Children's illnesses may go untreated and high rates of absenteeism from school are common.

Few children in crack families live with both parents, since marriages rarely survive the strain of the addict's drug use. Even if the crack-addicted parent remains in the home, many children of crack users grow up with little or no parental guidance. Dolores Bennett, a fifty-five-year-old woman in Detroit who manages a neighborhood home for homeless kids of crack families, notes: "Most of these children don't have someone in their house who takes care of them and shows them they love them. Most of the children are taking care of themselves."[23]

Children who remain with an addicted parent often assume the additional stress of hiding family problems from outsiders. Pressured to maintain secrecy, children tend to avoid seeking the help they need. Failure to find needed psychological help often leaves children feeling insecure, frustrated, and angry. According to child psychologists, children often feel that they are the cause of their parent's irrational and dysfunctional behavior. Children of crack addicts suffer from mistrust of others, difficulty with emotional expression, and failed intimate relationships. Without treatment, all of these problems carry over into adulthood.

Crack-Related Illnesses

As destructive as crack is to the addict's family, the drug is even more destructive to the health of the addict. Medical complications resulting from long-term crack use show up daily in emergency rooms across America. Cardiac arrest, strokes, and liver failure are all well-documented results of crack use. In addition to illness and deaths directly linked to crack use, numerous indirect or secondary illnesses are linked to it as well.

Some of these illnesses are commonly found among those who take drugs intravenously. Although crack is usually smoked, intravenous crack use is common in crack houses. Addicts tend to share needles, meaning that they risk contracting diseases such as HIV/AIDS and hepatitis, a severe liver inflammation. Nobody knows for sure how many crack addicts contract AIDS in this fashion,

Crack Addict

Three women addicted to crack—Teresa Wiltz, Diana Donnell, and Mia Mann—contributed an article to the April 1996 issue of *Essence* magazine called "Kicking Crack." In the article Donnell tells the following story of her desperate experiences on the road to crack addiction:

The first time I used crack, I was driving through the back roads with my girlfriend. At first I would just lace some weed with crack. Then weed disappeared from the street. You couldn't find marijuana anywhere, only crack. I knew I was hooked when I would do everything and anything for it. I took great pride in paying for my own drugs. I'd haul scrap iron. I'd sew. I felt like as long as I worked hard and paid for my own drugs, it was nobody's business what I did. But my judgment was off, way off.

I stole my grandfather's checks, and I got into some legal trouble because of it. I'm still paying restitution. The last year I used, I was almost killed three times. One man was strangling me until, gasping for air, I agreed to let him rape me. After that I started selling my body. Being in a small town, you know who the tricks [men who use prostitutes] are. And they know to come looking for you when they get paid. Then in 1988, my only girlfriend, my best friend all my life, was brutally murdered in Baton Rouge over some cocaine. The first thing people said when they heard about it was, "They got Juanita, Diana's next." That made me angry. I felt like I had to use even more to show people not everyone would die from using crack.

I was totally frustrated and alone. I didn't care what I looked like. I was worshiping the drug that had become my god, my man, my friend. From the time I woke up until the time I went to bed, I put all my efforts into smoking. I was a connoisseur. I could always tell what it was cut [diluted] with. When I would buy my rocks I would taste them, touch them with my tongue. Dealers didn't like that, but I didn't care. I wanted to know what I was getting.

But at some point you have to stop. Your body gives out on you. You can only get so high. When you try to get past the high, you become despicable, oblivious to the people around you.

but according to the National Institute on Drug Abuse (NIDA), use and abuse of illicit drugs, including crack, have become the leading risk factors for new cases of HIV infection. NIDA also reports that hepatitis is spreading rapidly among intravenous drug users.

A Particular Problem for Women and Children

In assessing health problems associated with crack, public health officials paint a bleaker picture for women than for men. NIDA maintains that crack can interfere with judgment and therefore lead to risky sexual behavior. Women addicts are particularly at risk because they are often forced to resort to prostitution to pay for their drugs. It is not unusual for female crack addicts to spend their entire day in crack houses trading sex for crack perhaps a dozen times. Even women who manage to avoid turning to prostitution are still at risk of contracting sexually transmitted diseases because rape is a common occurrence in crack houses.

Of even greater concern to society has been the fate of children born to crack-addicted women. Although initial fears among health professionals that such children would suffer severe and permanent brain damage have since proved unfounded, so-called crack babies do face some risks.

Perhaps the greatest of these risks is exposure to HIV/AIDS, which can be transmitted from an infected mother to her baby, either before or during childbirth or later through breast-feeding. Timely treatment of a pregnant HIV-positive patient with potent drugs like AZT or protease inhibitors can prevent this kind of transmission in many cases, but the same factors that keep crack addicts from seeking help—poverty and fear of the police—often keep the pregnant crack addict from getting the care that could prevent the infection of her baby with the deadly virus.

The many tragedies of crack use are dark realities of the crack and cocaine industry. The thousands of tragic stories surrounding cocaine and crack are not just the actions of addicts, but also the result of the actions of myriad people throughout the Western Hemisphere who make up a far-flung cocaine partnership.

Chapter 4

The Cocaine Partnership

The cocaine route that begins in the coca fields along the slopes of the Andes and ends five thousand miles away in thousands of American cities is a route built and maintained by an illicit and often violent cocaine partnership. Millions of workers are involved in producing and shipping the cocaine that eventually finds its way to still more millions of users in the United States. Most of those involved in this cocaine partnership will never meet although they all support this multibillion-dollar-a-year industry in many different ways and at many different levels.

All nations involved in the cocaine trade repudiate the drug. Yet that trade continues to flourish despite attempts to stop it. The success of this multinational illicit partnership in spite of Herculean efforts over three decades to destroy it is a complex and fascinating story.

Effects on the South American Economy

Ironically, the cocaine that causes or worsens poverty in the United States at the end of its journey north has provided an escape from poverty for more than a million South American peasants who participate in the cocaine trade in various ways. Before cocaine's popularity in the 1970s, most South American peasants earned a meager living growing such crops as coffee, bananas, citrus fruits, and various vegetables. Farmers were lucky if they made enough money to feed their families. During the 1970s, however, when consumption of cocaine, and demand for the drug, skyrocketed in the United States, the price of the drug escalated. The price for coca leaves also rose. Struggling farmers were quick to plant coca instead of traditional food crops to take advantage of this chance to escape poverty.

The lure of cocaine profits has created an economic and cultural revolution along the spine of the Andes. Cocaine's price escalation created a flood of hundreds of thousands of peasants from other regions inundating the fertile valleys of the Andes. Thirty years later, America's continuing demand for cocaine creates an incentive for peasants to abandon their fruit and coffee plantations, in favor of the more lucrative coca plants. And it is not just peasants who are attracted to the cocaine trade. Even educated professionals like schoolteachers have migrated into these

A coca plantation in Peru. Thousands of South American peasants have escaped poverty by replacing their fruit and coffee crops with more lucrative coca plants.

prime valleys because their modest salaries are well below what they can make owning and harvesting coca bushes.

Although coca provides a comparatively generous living for these farmers, growing and harvesting an illegal crop for export to the United States requires greater sophistication and organization than they can provide. Coordinating the efforts of so many individuals requires the financial and organizational muscle of the cocaine cartels.

Cartels

The three largest cocaine cartels, or groups organized to control coca production and limit competition, are the Medellín, Cali, and Cartagena, named after the major Colombian cities where several families control the cocaine trade, but each of the major cocaine-producing South American countries has several other cartels which compete to produce, manufacture, and export as much cocaine as possible to the United States and Europe.

Cartels are run and organized like any large corporation, though they operate illegally. They employ presidents or bosses, mid- and low-level managers, accountants, attorneys, security officers, and hundreds of thousands of general workers, all of whom support the growth, manufacture, distribution, and sale of cocaine. In a radio interview, a former member of the Medellín cartel gave the following response to the questions of how cartels are organized and how a person gets a job with one:

> Well, you don't go to the Yellow Pages and look for "cartel employment." And in my case, I was fortunate and unfortunate to have grown up with Carlos Lehder, [whom] we all know as head of the Medellín cartel. But the Medellín cartel had heads of different departments. Carlos was in charge of transportation. He was a very good pilot himself, and he trained pilots and he trained them his way. The other sections are just like any other company. We have the *Roprada,* we have the people that have to do with the growing, with the cultivation of the coca leaf. And then we have another segment that goes into production, what we call the kitchens—*las cocinas*—in the jungles of Colombia and Bolivia. And then we have a segment that is more sophisticated and it has to do with Carlos and how we're going to load the airplanes, how we're going to take them, what aircraft we're going to purchase, how the planes are going to be fueled and refueled, and what routes are we going to take for a certain trip.[24]

Since the cocaine trade begins with and depends on the cultivation and harvesting of the coca leaf, the largest group that operates within the umbrella of a cartel is the coca farmers.

The Farmers

Cocaine's route to America begins in thousands of small villages high in the Andes. Farmers who grow and harvest coca are called *cocaleros.* They own and harvest, on average, five acres of coca bushes. One acre can support about five hundred bushes, each of which produces hundreds of leaves. Because coca grows so well in this environment, *cocaleros* harvest four to five crops a year. To keep up with the demand for cocaine in America and Europe, South American growers slashed and burned jungles to make way for more coca bushes and terraced the hillsides to maximize the amount of land available for cultivation. Despite this lucrative business, life for a coca grower is difficult. Claire Hargreaves, in her book *Snowfields,* interviews one coca farmer in Bolivia who describes the many obstacles to getting started:

> Finding a plot wasn't easy because the Chapare [Valley] was already full. . . . I found one plot . . . but it was poor quality and often got flooded so the crops were destroyed. Next I found a place down the road from here, but you could only get to it by crossing several rivers by canoe. Often our provisions and clothes fell in the water on the way. I had to go to La Paz to sort out the papers giving the land titles. That was expensive: I had to pay the bus fare and, on top, bribes to the right people.[25]

Colombian workers gather coca leaves. South American coca farmers harvest four to five crops a year on an average of five acres.

Once in the village, the men who carry the coca leaves to market, called *zepes*, or ants, seek out the middlemen, or *pichicateros*, who buy the leaves. Prices fluctuate with demand, like other commodities. When the price of coca leaves is high, *cocaleros* can bring in $5,000 annually per acre; when prices are low, a farmer might earn one-tenth that amount.

The cocaine trade has been a boon to many South American villagers who grow and harvest the coca plants, and this is one reason it has been so difficult to eliminate at its source. Some of the taxes paid by the farmers finds its way back into the village and helps pay for schools, roads, simple hospitals, and other community-related improvements. These tax revenues are in addition to money the local cartel bosses hand out to the village mayors. The bosses do this in return for the mayors' guarantee to provide protection from the police and to encourage farmers to increase coca production.

The Manufacturers

The picked leaves are bundled into one-hundred-pound bags and carried to the local village on the backs of the *zepes*. The *zepes* are paid $2 to $3 a day plus food along with as many coca leaves as they want for their own consumption. The *zepes* arrive at local villages at night to avoid being robbed by bandits working for rival cartels and to avoid corrupt police officers, who force them to pay a bribe to pass.

The *pichicateros* who have purchased the coca leaves turn them over to the cartel's manufacturers to begin the process of converting the leaves into cocaine. The first step is to dig pits where coca is extracted from the leaves.

Coca extraction requires a pit to be near a river because water is an important ingredient in the process. Peasant workers line the pit with sheets of plastic and fill it with a mixture of coca leaves, sulfuric acid, kerosene, water, and lime. A cartel chemist mixes these ingredients in carefully prescribed amounts. Next, young men called stompers get in the pits barefooted and for twelve to fourteen hours they stomp and smash the concoction into a paste.

Six to ten stompers work a pit and each is paid between $10 and $15 a night. Hargreaves interviewed several stompers who describe the process:

> You need something inside of you to help you *bailar* (dance). We call it dancing because the whole thing turns into kind of a ritual: we stomp the leaves to the rhythm of music which we play on a cassette-recorder. Sometimes it's local Bolivian music. I and my friends prefer American rock. . . . We keep ourselves going by chewing coca leaves all night. It stops you feeling hungry or thirsty while you are working and keeps you awake. Some guys smoke cocaine paste while they work. Their bosses give it to them as part of their payment: it keeps them in business if they can get the boys addicted. The boys fall into sort of a trance. . . . Usually we work 12-hour stints, but sometimes the boss tells us to carry on until the process is finished. By day we'd crash out in the jungle, if possible on a bamboo bed to avoid the snakes.[26]

The cartel bosses also employ hundreds of additional workers needed for making the paste. *Zepes* transport the chemicals and plastic, chemists mix the chemicals in the pits, lookouts keep the police away, and cooks feed the entire crew. The cartel bosses stay

Workers called stompers use their bare feet to smash into a paste a mixture of coca leaves, sulfuric acid, kerosene, water, and lime.

away from the actual production of the paste to avoid the possibility of arrest by drug agents or attack by assassins working for rival cartels. Instead, they hire young boys as runners to give instructions to the workers and to pay them.

Colombia's Cocaine Violence

Cocaine-related violence is not restricted to the streets of America. All of the South American countries involved in cocaine production experience related violence. Nowhere else, however, has the level of bombings and public shootings exceeded that in Colombia, as cartel drug lords duel for control of cocaine production and export. In 1993 Bob Edwards, host of National Public Radio's (NPR) *Morning Edition*, interviewed reporter David Welna about daily cocaine violence in Colombia. Welna reports:

> On a Bogotá radio station, the news is about a 69-year-old newspaper publisher assassinated the night before in a provincial capital. As he got out of his car in front of his house, another car raced up and three gunmen opened fire. Five bullets killed the man instantly, while his wife and daughter looked on in horror. It's the kind of murder that makes news in Colombia

Cocaine-related violence is far worse in Colombia than in any other South American country.

for maybe a day or so, then gets lost under a new avalanche of killings. . . . There's no mystery about Colombia's violence. Colombia's prosecutor general recently blamed the government's eight-month-long failure to capture Pablo Escobar on three factors he said predominate in the country—incompetence, cowardice, and corruption. Meanwhile, Colombians are doing what they can to escape the violence. Some ride in bulletproof vehicles, others contract shotgun-toting security guards, and still others save money for a ticket to Miami.

These remote processing stations have the look of armed camps. Cartel armed guards thoroughly inspect all suspicious vehicles because the quantities of cocaine can easily add up to a ton and might be stolen or confiscated. Guards are primarily on the lookout for theft by rival cartels, although they also must be on guard to protect their contraband from corrupt police or from honest federal drug enforcement officers. These guards are inclined to shoot first and ask questions later. On a few occasions, innocent tourists wishing to visit rural villages have been suspected of being narcotic agents and have been shot and killed.

Some of these labs are capable of processing large amounts of cocaine and require a significant investment to set up and operate. To avoid capture by rivals or confiscation by police, labs are built on truck beds so they can be hidden deep into remote jungle sites and, if necessary, quickly moved.

When the stompers are done, the leaves are pressed and discarded and the remaining watery mixture, rich with the cocaine alkaloid, is siphoned off into square molds and dried until it forms a paste that is 40 percent pure cocaine. The paste, which is worth between $125 and $250 a pound, is transported by heavily armed guards to a central point run by the cartel for final processing, which involves treating the paste with hydrochloric acid and drying it to create cocaine powder.

Once the final processing is complete, the cocaine is packaged into one-kilogram bricks, each marked with a stamp identifying the cartel that produced it. Five hundred bricks are then placed on a small plane, which flies them to major cities where the highest-ranking cartel managers take charge of it. In its pure final form, the cocaine is priced at between $600 and $1,200 per pound.

The Distributors

The final step in the cocaine cartel's operation is to bring the cocaine bricks into the United States. This is by far the riskiest part of the business because it involves smuggling the cocaine past American customs agents. To move an estimated one thousand tons of cocaine annually requires a complex transportation strategy involving land, air, and sea operations.

A farmer spreads out cocaine paste that has been treated with hydrochloric acid. Once dried, the paste will become a powder that will be packaged in one-kilogram bricks and shipped around the world.

The land route involves trucking the cocaine north through Central America and Mexico. The cartel bosses know that no government agency in any nation has the money or manpower to inspect all of the thousands of trucks that move north along the Pan American Highway every day. Truck caravans under heavy guard carry as much as fifteen tons of cocaine at a time. Eventually, these shipments of cocaine are broken down into myriad small quantities and smuggled across the border in shipments of manufactured goods and agricultural products, as well as in suitcases and hidden compartments in automobiles.

For sheer speed and efficiency, however, airplanes are the favored mode of transportation. The Medellín cartel, for example, maintains its own fleet of several dozen aircraft to fly cocaine into Mexico, the Caribbean Islands, California, Florida, Texas, and as far north as New York. In the early days, the aircraft were twin-engined propeller planes, but as demand and production increased, the cartel used intermediaries to buy used Boeing 727s from commercial airlines. The Medellín cartel mechanics removed the seats and were able to haul about eleven tons of cocaine per flight.

Flying directly into an American airport is a difficult and risky proposition. The aircraft must have proper documentation and clearances from American customs officials, which must be presented upon landing. To circumvent this problem, the cartels falsify documents. The easiest document to falsify is a flight plan showing that the craft has already landed once in a city within the United States. This meant that customs officials would have no reason to inspect the plane, since the plane would be presumed to have been already inspected. The necessary information for falsifying such documents is not readily available, so now the corrupting influence of the cartels' money is felt even in the United States. When a former member of the Medellín cartel was questioned about bribing American officials, he said:

> There's a very sophisticated distribution system that had to deal with—would help with American authorities that were corrupt, to a certain point. I mean, there were people at the FAA [Federal Aviation Administration] that facilitated flight routes and access to airports and information on—what do you call it?—altitudes and flight plans, so we could fly without radar detection [by] DEA or Customs. And, indeed, it was a very sophisticated process.[27]

To throw U.S. customs officials off guard, the cartels also ship cocaine by sea. Many tons of cocaine are concealed within legitimate

bulk shipments of various products and loaded onto freighters bound for American ports. Here the determination of customs officials comes up against the ingenuity of the smugglers. The cartels have been known to pack bricks of

Agents display roofing tiles that concealed 3,600 pounds of cocaine. The tiles were confiscated from a Venezuelan ship in Miami.

cocaine inside welded automotive parts assembled in South America, within large plastic bags of bananas, or inside sealed decorative ceramic pots. One clever smuggler made what appeared to be handicraft products out of cocaine that had been disguised to look like plaster.

The cartels also use speedboats that travel at night between Caribbean ports and Florida coastal towns. Built small so they can travel fast, the speedboats are unable to carry more than five to eight hundred pounds. Nonetheless, they are very effective at eluding customs officials.

Cartels have gone to unusual lengths to smuggle cocaine. Following a drug seizure at a port in Colombia, the former boss of the Medellín cartel, Pablo Escobar, decided to build remote-controlled submarines to smuggle cocaine. Roberto Escobar, Pablo's brother, said in an interview with the British newspaper the *Independent* that "the subs were not big, but every two or three weeks, each could ship around 1200 kilos [2640 pounds]. We built two. When one was coming back, the other was going out. From departure to arrival, they were controlled electronically." [28]

Highly sophisticated technology such as submarines stand in stark contrast to the hundreds of thousands of coca farmers slogging through the damp valleys of the Andes. Yet both are elements in cocaine's route to the United States. Coordinating the efforts of simple peasant farmers with high-tech submarines can only be accomplished because the cartel bosses, known as *cruceños*, are willing to go to almost any lengths to keep the drug flowing in the pipeline.

Cartel Bosses

All control over the operations of cocaine production and distribution rests in the hands of the cartel bosses. A handful of *cruceños* manage and control the complex operations of the cartels as the cocaine moves from the coca fields of the Andes to the streets of America's large cities. Yet to all appearances, these individuals have little or no direct contact with the drugs they market. The *cruceños* live in large cities far from the jungles and valleys of the Andes.

For all their detachment from the cocaine itself, the *cruceños* profit enormously from its sale. Some *cruceños* have been known to take in more than $1 billion a month. These cartel bosses enjoy lives of unrestrained opulence protected behind the walls of well-guarded multimillion-dollar palatial estates rivaling those of the world's wealthiest families. According to an interview with

Pablo Escobar

Of the many cocaine cartel bosses in South America, none is more notorious than Pablo Escobar, who headed the Medellín cartel from the beginning of the 1980s until a Colombian security force of three thousand agents tracked him down following an eighteen-month manhunt and killed him in 1993 at the age of forty-four.

Escobar was considered the godfather of the South American cocaine trade. During the 1980s, he controlled three-quarters of all cocaine produced and shipped to the United States, at the time amounting to about six hundred tons annually. Members of Escobar's cartel estimate that he personally made a million dollars a day. This fortune paid for a lavish lifestyle for himself and his family, his personal bodyguard of 250 loyal supporters, and bribes to police and government officials.

Escobar's reign of terror encompassed the deaths of hundreds of low-level rivals all the way up to top national officials. He is blamed for the deaths of three Colombian presidential candidates and eleven of the nation's supreme court justices. Escobar was so willing to use violence that he bombed an airliner, killing 107 passengers because 7 of his enemies were on board. During the last year of his life, he was blamed for the deaths of nearly 500 police and drug agents who were trying to capture him.

Despite the trail of murder that followed Escobar, thousands hailed him as a savior of the poor. Escobar grew up in poverty and gave large sums of money to help the poor. He was known among his loyal followers for building four hundred homes, providing millions of dollars for soccer fields and uniforms, and for providing employment for tens of thousands of poor Colombians. Many in the city of Medellín revered him as a modern-day Robin Hood who stole from the rich and gave to the poor.

The governments of Colombia and the United States celebrated his death with the hope that it would reduce the production and flow of cocaine into the United States. To the common people of Medellín, however, his death represented the end of a man who helped them out of their poverty. Since his death, tens of thousands of Colombia's poor visit his tomb annually and rub his tombstone for good luck.

David Welna, a reporter in Colombia, "They send their children to Ivy League schools in the States, and people say they fancy themselves the Kennedys and Rockefellers of Latin America." [29] Cartel bosses travel about their cities in the most expensive imported luxury cars on their way to the finest restaurants and resorts. Many own multiple homes in many of the world's major cities that serve as vacation estates and as potential safe havens should they ever need to take refuge from authorities in South America.

Although the life styles of the *cruceños* may appear glamorous, there is a deadly downside to this occupation. Cartel bosses have many enemies within rival cartels and are also subject to arrest by various law enforcement agencies. Wherever the bosses go, bodyguards armed with the latest fully automatic weapons accompany them. This same protection is extended to family members as well. In addition to bodyguards, family cars are custom fitted with bulletproof windows

Notorious cartel boss Pablo Escobar poses with his wife in 1983. Escobar headed the Medellín cartel until he was hunted down and killed in 1993 by Colombian agents.

and doors, and the undercarriages are reinforced to withstand bomb blasts. To achieve the same sense of security in their estates, ten-foot-high walls enclose their houses and the latest electronic monitoring devices announce the presence of intruders.

Much of the wealth that these men acquire is spent on bribes to the police and to politicians in their home countries, and corruption surrounding the cocaine trade in many South American countries is rampant. Newspaper publishers are also occasionally paid off to ensure that the press does not report on the drug lords' activities, and should bribery fail, threats and occasional assassinations are considered standard business practices. Some of the money made by the cartel bosses goes to helping their friends and family members get elected to high political office to ensure their own protection. On rare occasions when all these measures fail and someone is arrested, they hire the best lawyers money can buy. By one tactic or another, most *cruceños* who are arrested avoid prison sentences.

American Dealers and Users

The final members of the cocaine "family" are the American dealers and users. When the cocaine arrives in America, it is sold to high-level distribution bosses in large metropolitan centers. At this point, most of the influence of the South American cocaine cartels ends. From this point forward, the bulk cocaine is parceled out to lower-level distribution networks that supply communities throughout America. Much of the American distribution is controlled by criminal organizations operating in the United States or in Mexico. (Mexico does not grow coca or manufacture cocaine, but since a great deal of the South American cocaine travels through Mexico on its way to America, Mexicans are involved in its smuggling and distribution.) According to a National Narcotics Intelligence Consumers Committee (NNICC) report:

> In recent years, this infrastructure [American cocaine traffickers] has become heavily dependent on the smuggling services of drug gangs operating from Mexico, which has enabled the drug gangs there to emerge as sophisticated and powerful international drug trafficking organizations within their own right. These powerful gangs, for example, have increased their involvement in the distribution of cocaine in the United States on their own initiative and in concert with the Colombian mafias.[30]

Once the cocaine reaches big cities, some is processed into crack and the rest is divided into one-ounce or one-gram packets. These small quantities of cocaine are easily shipped throughout the United States concealed in automobiles or in suitcases and loaded on buses or airplanes. Some is even packaged and shipped through the mail.

The high-level dealers are the ones who profit the most from the cocaine trade in the United States. The average cost of each one-kilogram brick of cocaine they purchase is about $23,000. They divide the brick into thirty-five one-ounce packets that they sell for about $1,200 each. Sometimes, to make even more profit, they will dilute, or "cut," the pure cocaine with harmless white powder substances such as baby powder to stretch the brick to forty-five one-ounce packets. On the street, each one-ounce pack is divided into twenty-eight one-gram packets, which sell for about $100 apiece.

Although the cocaine industry has raised the standard of living for hundreds of thousands of peasants in South America, the end result in America has been a virtual tidal wave of violence, misery, and poverty on American streets. America's law enforcement agencies, therefore, use a variety of strategies to seize cocaine before it finds it way to the users.

Chapter 5

Cocaine Interdiction

Suppression of the cocaine trade has been one of the American government's objectives since 1914, when Congress outlawed its general use. In the 1970s, however, other American social institutions joined forces with law enforcement agencies to stem the use of cocaine. Today, in addition to the federal government, organizations as diverse as churches and synagogues, schools and universities, youth and national health organizations, and organized sports have programs in place to discourage the use of cocaine and crack. Still, it remains the job of various law enforcement agencies to capture and jail those who sell the drug and to intercept and seize shipments of cocaine.

Much success has resulted from the work of these government and community groups. The National Household Survey on Drug Abuse (NHSDA) estimates that in 1985, at the height of the cocaine epidemic, 5.7 million people used cocaine, 3.1 million of whom were frequent users. By 1998, however, the number had dropped to 1.8 million current users of whom an estimated 595,000 were frequent users.

In spite of this success, there remains much reason for concern. Although current numbers reflect a decline from the highs of

1985, the decline leveled off in 1991 and use of cocaine has remained steady ever since. Of greater concern is the fact that among teenagers and college students, the rate of use is actually increasing.

In response to the growth in use of cocaine by younger people, the government has redoubled its efforts to keep drugs from ever reaching the United States. The official strategy involves stopping the production of cocaine in South America as well as stopping its use in America.

Eradicating the Coca Crop

Many American government officials believe that the best way to end the American cocaine epidemic is to eradicate the coca crops in South America. This logic seems unassailable although implementing such a strategy is far from simple. Hundreds of thousands of South American farmers derive their livelihood from coca harvests. In the minds of the peasant farmers, coca production is not an issue of growing illegal drugs, it is an issue of feeding their families. In addition to the farmers, hundreds of thousands of South Americans derive their income from the other jobs within the cocaine cartels as manufacturers, transporters, packagers,

Peruvian peasants transport coca leaves. Hundreds of thousands of South American peasants rely on coca crops to earn a living.

bodyguards, and distributors. Most of the peasant workers believe that without the cocaine industry, the quality of their lives will decline. Some government officials in cocaine-producing nations— at least privately—agree. Besides, they argue, the drug problem is caused by consumption in the United States, not by production in South America.

The U.S. government is not alone in calling for the elimination of the coca bushes from the Andes. Many influential South Americans as well as some government leaders also support the idea. These people recognize that although cocaine generates more income for farmers than legal crops do, the industry also encourages widespread corruption. Moreover, the violence that accompanies the cocaine trade can be extreme. Over several years in the early 1990s, for example, Colombian officials linked about twenty thousand deaths a year to the cocaine business.

Because of the problems caused by cocaine addiction in America and the negative effects of the cocaine industry in South American nations, government officials of all involved countries have united to curb coca production. Two different strategies have been attempted. One is to replace the coca crops with profitable food crops; the other is to use national military forces to attack the cocaine supply line directly.

Crop Replacement

The climate in which coca thrives is suitable for many food crops as well. The U.S. government, in concert with several South American governments, has attempted to assist coca growers in planting alternative crops such as bananas, coffee, citrus, pepper, pineapples, and several varieties of beans. The assistance comes in the form of better seed, new farming techniques, and millions of dollars for irrigation and disease control. Don Alejandro Campos, a farmer in the Peruvian interior, was one of the first to receive aid: "They brought me better seeds, beans, bananas, corn, citrus fruits, and they helped me cure my sick plants." [31]

In addition to agricultural assistance, the United States has directly paid farmers a one-time subsidy of $1,000 for each acre of coca destroyed. This incentive had little initial success because the price paid for coca leaves was so high and the farmers could make more than $1,000 per acre by keeping the land planted in coca. Later, however, when the price of coca fell, thousands of farmers applied for the money to destroy their coca fields.

The success of crop replacement has been limited. The immediate problem with this approach is that even at reduced prices, coca brings in more money per pound than food crops. For example, in the years 1999 and 2000, the price for coca leaves fluctuated between $1 and $2 a pound. By comparison, coffee usually brings farmers 50 cents a pound, and bananas 10 cents a pound.

A second problem with the alternate crop strategy is opposition from the cartels. The cartels send messengers to encourage the farmers to grow coca. The cartels also encourage coca growing by providing their own form of assistance to farmers. Canadian journalist Tom Fennell, who traveled to Peru to interview coca farmers, reports that one farmer told him, "The farmers who sell coca to drug traffickers have fewer transport problems than the ones who cultivate coffee, citrus fruits and bananas. The drug traffickers come right into the jungle to pick up the coca."[32]

Moreover, cartels also have a history of violence when peaceful agreement with the farmers cannot be reached. Cartel enforcers have been known to threaten and even murder banana growers as well as foreigners assisting farmers in growing the alternative crops. Not surprisingly, many farmers get the message and continue to grow coca.

Finally, the biggest problem with the crop replacement policy is that even as some farmers reduced their cultivation of coca plants, others planted more. The result is that the crop replacement programs have not significantly reduced cocaine production.

Policies such as crop replacement have put many South American governments in a bind. Most governments support crop replacement, believing that in the end, growing food is better for the moral and economic health of their countries than growing coca. These governments are also keenly aware that by supporting crop replacement and other anticocaine policies, they stand to receive more foreign aid from the United States. The cartels, on the other hand, are opposed to any policies that reduce coca production and willingly use violence to end those policies. The violence, in the form of assassinations of various government officials, has cost thousands of lives.

For the most part, governments of coca-producing nations have accepted American aid. The amounts can be substantial. For example, in 2000, President Bill Clinton and the U.S. Congress authorized $1.9 billion to help Colombia equip and train anti-drug armies.

Military Assault

Many officials of the U.S. government believe that an all-out military assault on cartels is the only solution to the cocaine epidemic in the United States. Large sums have been appropriated for the purchase of dozens of military helicopters, numerous lightweight

A member of an elite antidrug unit of Colombia's National Police watches an airplane dump herbicide on an illicit coca crop.

assault vehicles, assault rifles, and training for Colombian anti-narcotic troops. This strategy has three objectives: eradicate the coca crops, drive the cartel armies away from the coca fields, and arrest the cartel bosses.

To accomplish the first objective, Colombian government pilots flying American supply planes sprayed the coca fields with millions of gallons of herbicides. Although this killed vast tracts of coca plants, the tactic also killed food crops. Moreover, the herbicides made peasant families living and working in the fields sick. Well-armed cartel ground forces complicated the eradication campaign by shooting at the planes as they flew overhead.

The second tactic of Colombian antinarcotic troops was to force their way deep into well-guarded coca plantations to disrupt harvests and manufacturing. Once deep in the jungles, government troops using assault vehicles and high-powered weapons fought cartel forces. After driving off the cartel's guards, the troops cut down the coca plants and set them on fire. This tactic of quick strikes caught some cartel guards by surprise, resulting in their capture. Most, however, had been warned in advance of the assaults and fled to safety. The strike teams, moreover, could only uproot and burn a relatively small number of coca bushes in a single assault.

The third and most difficult tactic was to capture and imprison as many of the high-level cartel bosses as possible, on the theory that without strong leaders the cartels would disintegrate. The primary focus during the 1990s was the head of the Medellín cartel, Pablo Escobar, who was known to control as much as three-quarters of the Colombian cocaine business. A Colombian strike force captured and imprisoned Escobar, but after only six months in a specially built prison described by many observers as more of a resort than a jail, Escobar walked out and disappeared. Escobar was eventually located and killed after an eighteen-month manhunt.

Although Escobar was eliminated and the Medellín cartel suffered a setback as a result, the Colombian government did not enjoy a lasting victory. Rival cartels and drug lords quickly stepped in to replace Escobar. In an article published in the *Economist* magazine shortly after Escobar was killed, a staff writer reported,

> In Colombia, the DEA [Drug Enforcement Administration] says that Cali has replaced Medellín as the center of the industry and supplies roughly three-quarters of the cocaine reaching the United States. But several other important trafficking organizations have emerged. As well as re-organized remnants of the Medellín organization, they include outfits based on Colombia's north coast, in other areas of the Cauca valley near Cali, in the eastern plains and in Bogotá, the capital.[33]

As new *cruceños* stepped forward to replace Escobar, America's policy makers in Washington, D.C., realized that to achieve greater success, high-level South American politicians had to cooperate more fully with the United States. Securing that cooperation required a combination of incentives like crop replacement and military aid, and

President Bill Clinton and Colombian president Andres Pastrana exchange documents after signing a declaration of an alliance against illegal drugs in 1998.

pressure in the form of threats to cut off other aid that many South American governments had come to rely on.

The Certification Policy

In part, the motive behind increasing the pressure on the cocaine-exporting nations was the fact that at least some of the monetary aid disappeared into the pockets of government officials without producing any measurable reduction on cocaine production.

The pressure the United States exerted came in the form of a policy called certification, which is an annual assessment of antidrug efforts in countries where drugs are produced for export to America. If the president of the United States finds that a foreign government is acting diligently to stem the flow of drugs, that nation is certified as supportive of America's antidrug foreign policy and receives substantial foreign aid in return. Most South American governments depend on the foreign aid to keep their economies stable and attempt to qualify for certification as a result.

The certification program is controversial, however. Critics make the claim that the financial aid tied to certification is not actually used

by some South American governments to suppress cocaine production; rather, it is actually used to stifle political opposition. In Colombia, for example, the government is battling several rebel guerrilla forces. The largest and most well organized is called the Revolutionary Armed Forces of Colombia, or FARC. Critics charge that some of America's foreign aid tied to certification is being spent on military equipment that the Colombian government is using against the FARC.

U.S. and Colombian officials meet prior to an annual antinarcotics certification decision. In the background, police torch a cocaine processing facility.

Narco-Terrorists

A relatively new complication in the already complex political problems of South America is the emergence of revolutionary groups that finance their guerrilla wars with profits from cocaine production. Termed narco-terrorists by the press, these groups seek to overthrow several South American governments that are supported by the United States, further involving the United States in South American affairs.

In Colombia, the latest wrinkle in the ongoing attempt to stop cocaine production is the cooperation between the cocaine cartels and terrorists. This situation makes for strange bedfellows. Until 1997, the cartel bosses trafficked in cocaine strictly for profit. It was in their interest to have a stable government, even one opposed to the drug trade: Controlling the government through bribery, threats, and other forms of corruption was considered a cost of doing business. Now, however, cartels see potential benefits in supporting revolutionaries who will in turn support the cartels once in power.

The largest of the narco-terrorists is the Revolutionary Armed Forces of Colombia, or FARC. Its aim is to install a Marxist form of government that will seize all private industry in Colombia and distribute the nation's wealth evenly among all citizens. The U.S. government is concerned that should FARC be successful, Colombia's democracy might become a narco-state run by the FARC narco-terrorists and all attempts to shut down cocaine cartels will end.

In an interview in *High Times* magazine in July 1999, Representative Benjamin Gilman, chairman of the House International Relations Committee, said in reference to a possible peace plan between FARC and the Colombian government, "I am skeptical of a Colombian peace process that results in 16,000 square miles of territory being given to narco-guerrillas, who work hand-in-hand with the world's most dangerous drug dealers."

In the same interview, Marine Gen. Charles E. Wilhelm, head of the Miami-based U.S. Southern Command, which is training a 950-troop "counter-narcotics" battalion, said, "It is impossible to spray fields protected by the FARC without battling the rebels, a job assigned to the [Colombian] army. The army has been defeated in virtually every large-scale encounter with FARC, which pays its 15,000 troops three times what army conscripts make."

Little Change

Critics of the American government's efforts to eliminate cocaine at its source also point to the lack of overall change in levels of the drug's production. The results of the various attempts to reduce cocaine production in South America are reported in the State Department's annual report to Congress on international narcotics control. The report issued in 2000 indicated that land in coca production in Peru, Bolivia, and Ecuador had fallen about 15 percent compared with 1995 acreage. There was, however, one notable exception to the trend of declining coca production. As the number of acres of coca production declined in most South American countries, production doubled in Colombia, meaning the total acreage devoted to coca production had changed little. Coca production had merely migrated north.

Many American leaders debate the effectiveness of America's antidrug policies in South America. Although most support continuing the policy, few believe it is achieving reasonable reductions and all recognize that too much cocaine continues to be sold on American streets. For years, Congress has recognized the need for a second line of defense to regain control over the South American cocaine trade.

Border Seizures

The second line of defense for intercepting cocaine is the nation's airports, maritime ports, and points of entry along the Mexican and Canadian borders. U.S. customs officers are authorized to inspect any person, vehicle, container, or object that they suspect may conceal contraband such as cocaine. Seizing cocaine here—in theory, at least—is easier than trying to convince foreign governments that they should destroy their lucrative coca crops.

News reports often dramatically chronicle the arrests of smugglers and seizures of cocaine. Customs officials and border patrol officers cite these seizures as evidence of America's success in the war on cocaine. Suitcases containing between twenty and thirty pounds of cocaine are routinely found. Cars crossing into the United States at Mexican border-crossing points sometimes contain as much as five hundred pounds of cocaine hidden in trunks or submerged in gas tanks. Customs inspectors and Coast Guard crews occasionally find a ton or more of cocaine hidden among legitimate cargo aboard large container ships.

As drug and law enforcement agencies increased their vigilance at all points of entry, cocaine smugglers adopted increasingly sophisticated strategies to move their contraband. The cartels abandoned smuggling many small shipments in favor of fewer large ones. They purchased their own heavy aircraft to fly several tons at a time. During the 1980s, cartels landed their planes at small private airports in Florida, Texas, and California. However, when U.S. agents placed these airports under surveillance, smugglers turned to landing their planes on remote dirt roads.

To counter the smuggling threat from aircraft, the DEA added radar planes equipped with infrared cameras to detect, track, and intercept smugglers' aircraft. Military aircraft bristling with sophisticated detection devices began making flights from Florida and Texas deep into Mexican and Central American airspace to search for questionable aircraft flying north. When suspicious aircraft were spotted, their positions were radioed to intercept aircraft capable of following them to their destinations where they could be searched.

These sorts of aerial cat-and-mouse games sometimes end tragically. In April 2001, Peruvian military aircraft patrolling the boarder with Ecuador were directed by a U.S. surveillance plane to an unidentified single-engine plane entering Peruvian airspace. Suspecting the plane to be smuggling cocaine, one of the Peruvian jet fighters closed in and shot it down. Tragically, the small plane was carrying American missionaries, not cocaine, and the mistake took the lives of a mother and her seven-month-old child.

Mixed Results

The combined efforts to stop cocaine production have yielded results. In 1999, U.S. law enforcement agencies seized an estimated fifty-five tons of cocaine among all entry points. These seizures represent about 7 percent of all cocaine entering the United States. In addition to seizures at ports of entry, additional DEA-assisted seizures in Mexico accounted for another twenty-seven tons and seizures in several Caribbean islands accounted for another fifteen tons. Despite stepped-up patrols and improved intelligence, William Ledwith, chief of international operations for the DEA, testified before the congressional Subcommittee on Criminal Justice, Drug Policy, and Human

Resources that "the CNC [Crime and Narcotics Center] now estimates Colombia's potential 1999 cocaine production from Colombia's domestic coca crop to be 520 metric tons [573 tons], based on cultivation of 122,900 hectares [303,563 acres] of coca."[34] Reports from the Department of Defense, the Coast Guard, and other federal agencies estimate that eight hundred tons of cocaine flowed into the United States in 2000 from all of South America. Critics of the government's war on cocaine believe the actual amount is easily one thousand tons.

These statistics indicate that probably at least 88 percent of the cocaine shipped from South America finds it way to the United States. As one American critic of the war on cocaine puts it, trying to reduce the flood of cocaine into the United States is "like standing under a waterfall with a bucket."[35] Once cocaine is inside the country, a third and final line of defense attempts to seize the drug.

Seizures Within the United States

Once cocaine is inside the United States, preventing its distribution and use becomes dramatically more complicated. The sheer size of the nation and the number of people illegally involved with cocaine make completely preventing its delivery to users virtually impossible, although authorities continue to hope that new laws will provide them the tools they need to control the cocaine epidemic.

Although the laws governing cocaine are numerous, the majority are aimed at punishing those who are involved in selling drugs. In 1986, mandatory minimum sentences were passed requiring judges to impose specified jail sentences; then in 1988, the drug trafficking conspiracy law was passed to incarcerate officials of any businesses that in any way associate with cocaine traffickers. In 1999, the federal government's Kingpin Act targeted large-volume dealers by freezing their assets in the United States and by imposing legal sanctions against Americans who knowingly do business with them. All of these were primarily aimed at prosecuting and incarcerating high-level cocaine traffickers. The problem

Legalizing Cocaine and Crack

Although the majority of Americans favor the illegal status of cocaine and crack, not everyone shares this view. One of the most prominent advocates of legalization of cocaine and crack is Nobel Prize–winning economist Milton Friedman. In 1991, libertarian psychiatrist Thomas Szasz, a vocal opponent of drug control, interviewed Friedman for a radio broadcast called "America's Drug Forum," a transcript of which is available at the Schaffer Library of Drug Policy website. Szasz begins by asking Friedman how America would change with the legalization of drugs.

FRIEDMAN: I see America with half the number of prisons, half the number of prisoners, ten thousand fewer homicides a year, inner cities in which there's a chance for these poor people to live without being afraid for their lives, citizens who might be respectable who are now addicts not being subject to becoming criminals in order to get their drug, being able to get drugs for which they're sure of the quality.

SZASZ: Let us consider another drug then, and that is the drug crack.

FRIEDMAN: Crack would never have existed, in my opinion, if you had not had drug prohibition. Why was crack created? The preferred method of taking cocaine, which I understand was by sniffing it, snorting it, became very expensive and they [drug dealers] were desperate to find a way of packaging cocaine.

SZASZ: [Is not cocaine and crack drug dealing] in fact an enterprise which harms other persons?

FRIEDMAN: It does harm a great many other people, but primarily because it's prohibited. There are an enormous number of innocent victims now. You've got the people whose purses are stolen, who are bashed over the head by people trying to get enough money for their next fix. You've got the people killed in the random drug wars. You've got the corruption of the legal establishment. You've got the innocent victims who are taxpayers who have to pay for more and more prisons, and more and more prisoners, and more and more police. You've got the rest of us who don't get decent law enforcement because all the law enforcement officials are busy trying to do the impossible.

SZASZ: [What about] violence surrounding the drug trade?

FRIEDMAN: The violence is due to prohibition and nothing else. How much violence is there surrounding the alcohol trade? There's some, only because we prohibit the sale of alcohol to children, which we should do, and there's some because we impose very high taxes on alcohol and, as a result, there's some incentive for bootlegging. But there's no other violence around it.

with the laws, however, has been that even though offenders have been arrested under these laws, most tend to be local street dealers and users who also deal cocaine to support their own habits.

Studies assessing the effectiveness of these laws indicate that the high-level cocaine traffickers avoid handling the drugs themselves. Consequently, these high-level traffickers cannot be connected with the drugs. In a report issued in 1995, the U.S. Sentencing Commission found that only 11 percent of federal drug trafficking defendants

Drug lord Alberto Orlandez Gamboa is escorted by Colombian police prior to his extradition to the United States.

were major traffickers. As a result, most of the high-level traffickers remain in business.

Although the task of interdiction within the United States is a daunting one, agencies such as the DEA are experimenting with new tactics. In 1995, the Mobile Enforcement Team (MET) program was created to respond to the drug-related violent crime that plagues certain urban neighborhoods. Their value is their ability to quickly move narcotic agents housed in a mobile command unit, in the form of a trailer loaded with sophisticated communication equipment. The first 256 deployments of MET resulted in seizures of seventeen hundred pounds of cocaine.

The DEA, aware of the amount of cocaine shipped on the nation's highways, also initiated Operations Pipeline and Convoy, which targeted motor vehicles. Their strategy is to stop and inspect suspicious vehicles on the nation's highways. Agents look for cars riding low on their springs, suggesting they are carrying heavy loads, and truckers whose source and destination papers appear to be falsified. Between 1986 and 2000, Operations Pipeline and Convoy seized 293,000 pounds of cocaine and 2,000 pounds of crack. To further increase cocaine seizures, the DEA initiated the High Intensity Drug Trafficking Areas (HIDTA) program to reduce drug trafficking in areas identified as experiencing unusually high drug activity.

Despite the best efforts of the DEA and other government agencies at intercepting the supply and prosecuting traffickers, the amount of cocaine available on America's streets remains large. The success of the war on cocaine, therefore, is questioned by many who have studied the problem. These two observations have led many health-care professionals to conclude that there is little more that can be done to stop the problem except to offer treatment and recovery for those who are addicted.

Chapter 6

Treatment and Recovery

Cocaine treatment and recovery is a controversial issue for several reasons, all of which focus on the validity and effectiveness of various methods. The debate centers on questions such as whether addicts can really break their dependency on cocaine and whether any of the current therapies available to addicts has a high enough success rate to justify the $3.2 billion that the federal government annually spends on a variety of therapies.

Still, most American political and community leaders agree that cocaine and crack addicts who seek help should get it. The debate centers on determining the best strategy for curing the addict. This debate prompted the General Accounting Office (GAO) of the federal government to investigate the effectiveness of various therapies. In 1996 the GAO published the results of a lengthy study focused on cocaine that concluded that no one was sure exactly how much good therapy was doing:

> Although studies conducted over nearly 3 decades consistently show that treatment reduces drug use and crime, current data collection techniques do not allow accurate measurement of the extent to which treatment reduces the use of illicit drugs. Furthermore, research literature has not yet yielded definitive evidence to identify which approaches work best for specific groups of drug abusers.[36]

A recovering crack addict, who is in a drug treatment program and has been drug-free for nine months, hugs her children after regaining custody of them.

The conclusion of the GAO report that the best therapeutic approaches have not yet been identified prompted many specialists working in the field of drug rehabilitation to argue that no single therapy can be identified as being the best for all addicts and that the best strategy is for the addict and his or her therapist to explore several therapies. Experts have also concluded that whichever therapies are applied, the addict must understand that there are no short-term solutions to the complexities of addiction.

Recovery Is a Long-Term Commitment

Not only is there little agreement on which therapies work best, but even the goal of therapy is open to debate. One of the early lessons learned by therapists was that recovery from cocaine and crack addiction is more complicated than simple abstinence. Recovery, many experts say, is often a long-term process characterized by alternating periods of abstinence and use. In many cases, addicts may reduce cocaine consumption but never achieve complete abstinence.

Harm Reduction

A growing number of health-care professionals, after many years of experience, have adopted the view that some cocaine and crack users cannot be expected to end their drug use. Although this view is in conflict with principles of recovery therapy that assert that addicts can recover given enough time and different types of therapy, the popularity of the policy of harm reduction is growing.

Harm reductionists believe that the primary goal of the war on cocaine and crack should not be to eliminate their use or to arrest all users but rather to reduce the harm that the drugs cause. The harm reductionists also believe that chronic cocaine and crack users constitute a public health problem rather than a law enforcement problem.

Harm reductionists believe that those who can be persuaded to stop using the drugs should be, and that those who cannot be stopped should be encouraged to use cocaine and crack more safely. To that end, harm reductionists favor expanding the availability of needle-exchange programs and safe crack houses for IV cocaine and crack users, and establishing maintenance programs that provide addicts with a daily dose of the drug. Harm reductionists also attempt to avoid making moral judgments about cocaine and crack users while encouraging more tolerant public attitudes.

Harm reductionists have drawn sharp criticism, accused of blindness to the tremendous harm to innocent friends and family caused by cocaine and crack addiction. There is little hard evidence that harm reduction makes life easier for the families and friends of cocaine and crack users. Critics also believe that harm reductionists make too little effort to intervene between addicts and their drugs to force them to address the personal problems that cause their addictions.

How much therapy is needed has also been questioned. The initial belief that permanent recovery would quickly follow a week or two of abstinence proved incorrect. Studies have consistently shown that the minimum amount of time required to gain even minimal control over cocaine addiction is three months. Any period of therapy that lasted less than three months met with negligible success. The same studies have also confirmed that as treatment time increases, success rates also increase.

During the first three months of therapy, the primary focus is to produce initial withdrawal from cocaine as well as nutritional and emotional stabilization. Studies suggest that patients who are able to abstain from cocaine use for at least three weeks during the first three-month period improve their probability of being cocaine free one year later. Those who are able to abstain for the entire three months have a significantly better chance, although very few are able to abstain for three months.

The first three months is just a start. How long therapy must continue to achieve what can be termed success is difficult to predict. Interviews with addicts who complete therapy suggest some predictors of success. The three advantages that appear to contribute to the best results are full-time employment, education, and a stable childhood. Psychologists believe that these factors are predictors of success because each contributes to a positive and nurturing environment for the addict. Consequently, addicts who have none of the three often start and stop therapy many times over many years without ever conquering their habit.

Addicted individuals may require prolonged treatment and multiple episodes of treatment to achieve long-term abstinence and to restore their ability to function in society. Many therapists now believe that therapy must be continued on a regular basis for at least one year to achieve long-term abstinence and, for some addicts, therapy may need to continue for the remainder of their lives.

With the understanding that therapy will last a long time, the next issue for the therapist to consider is the type or types of therapies that best suit the addict.

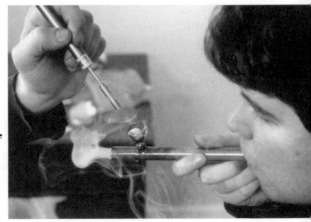

On the road to recovery, many crack addicts are unable to completely abstain from taking the drug and experience frequent relapses.

The Strategy of Multiple Therapies

Cocaine and crack addiction is a complex problem, so it is perhaps not surprising that therapy is equally complex and requires multiple strategies. The multiple therapy approach usually begins with a form of individual therapy called psychotherapy in which addicts discuss problems from their past that may have played a role in their addiction. After a few weeks or months, cognitive therapy might begin, which focuses on teaching patients to generate positive thoughts about themselves, their personal strengths, and their ability to quit cocaine. Next, a behavioral approach might be used to

The Cycle of Cocaine Addiction

Drug abuse therapists have identified what they believe to be a consistent and predictable cycle of cocaine addiction. The therapists at Narconon International, a drug abuse rehabilitation center in Los Angeles, specialize in cocaine and crack addiction. Their Narconon website, posts an electronic brochure that summarizes the following six steps in the cycle of addiction:

1. The life cycle of addiction begins with a problem, discomfort, or some form of emotional or physical pain a person is experiencing. The situation appears to have no healthy solution.

2. This person tries cocaine or some other drug to ease the discomfort. Initially, the cocaine appears to solve the problem and it gains value as an apparent cure.

3. The person uses it repeatedly with the same curative effect. Getting more of the drug now becomes more important than solving the problem that first prompted the cocaine use. Now the person is trapped.

4. The user now must conceal his or her use from friends and family members. Lies and self-deception about possible addiction leads to guilt and withdrawal from others and a life of isolation begins.

5. Cocaine becomes the user's only friend. Nothing has a higher priority than guaranteeing a steady supply of cocaine. Schoolwork or job performance suffers and gradually the user either quits or is dismissed. Crime commonly begins as a means to pay for drugs.

6. In addition to the embarrassment of the downhill slide and unethical behavior, the person's body now craves cocaine. The user is now obsessed with getting and using this drug, and will do anything to avoid the pain of withdrawal. The ability to get "high" decreases as the user's body adapts to the cocaine. He or she must take more and more in this downward spiral. The invisible line of addiction has been crossed and the person is now a cocaine addict.

improve daily function and positive activities such as finding a job, associating with drug-free friends, and avoiding old hangouts associated with drug use. Finally, several sessions of group therapy involving several people sharing their experiences with cocaine recovery might be recommended. Counselors hope that after exposure to a mix of therapies each patient will have found valuable tools to aid his or her recovery.

Dr. Jack Blaine, of NIDA's Division of Treatment Research and Development, notes in reference to the multiple-therapy strategy, "These results underline the valuable role of well-designed drug counseling in treating drug abuse. More specifically, this study demonstrates the effectiveness that combined counseling therapies can have in treating cocaine addiction."[37]

As an individual's treatment progresses, the addict's situation must be assessed continually and treatment modified as necessary to ensure that the therapy meets the person's changing needs. For many patients, alternating from one strategy to another in a prescribed sequence assists the addict in abstaining from cocaine use. To successfully time therapy changes, the therapist looks for the moment the patient is in need of new motivation to introduce the next strategy. It is always considered better to slow down and work at a pace that is comfortable and productive for a particular individual than to change strategies too quickly.

The wide variety of cocaine treatment and recovery therapies in use today collectively produce a recovery rate of somewhere between 15 and 25 percent, depending upon which agencies are reporting the results. When they develop their strategies, therapists draw on a variety of individual therapies, group therapies, and medication therapies and create a treatment plan tailored to a particular addict's needs.

Individual Treatments

Individual treatments are, as the name implies, therapy sessions in which one therapist works with only one patient at a time. Individual therapies usually include behavioral therapies that offer people strategies for coping with their drug cravings, teaching them ways to avoid drugs, preventing relapse, and helping them deal with relapse if it occurs. The three most common approaches are psychotherapy, behavioral, and cognitive.

According to Dr. Lewis R. Wolberg, psychotherapy is

the treatment, by psychological means, of problems of an emotional nature in which a trained person deliberately establishes a professional relationship with the patient with the object of (1) removing, modifying, or retarding existing symptoms, (2) mediating disturbed patterns of behavior, and (3) promoting positive personality growth and development.[38]

As applied to the treatment of cocaine addiction, psychotherapy typically involves an addict discussing his or her emotional and behavioral problems with the therapist. The objective is twofold: to achieve an understanding of the causes of the addiction and to change the addict's thoughts, feelings, and behavior. Generally, the patient does most of the talking and is always encouraged to discuss dreams and memories of childhood experiences.

Like psychotherapy, behavioral therapy focuses on the behavior that is causing the addiction, but unlike psychotherapy, it does not involve discussing childhood experiences. Instead, the objective of behavior therapy is to focus on observable everyday behavior and on techniques to change maladaptive habits. Change takes place within the addict by techniques such as relaxation, curing phobias that may in part be related to the addiction, and the use of aversion therapy that inflicts various forms of discomfort when the patient behaves the wrong way.

Cognitive therapy focuses on changing addicts' thoughts about themselves and their addictions. The objective is to rid them of unreasonably negative thoughts about themselves and to replace those thoughts with positive ones. Very often cocaine addicts harbor distorted or irrational thoughts that must be corrected before addiction can be cured. Examples are thinking that minor setbacks are catastrophic, that their lives are worse than any other person's, and that everyone else is smarter and happier. Once patients realize that such extreme irrational thinking is flawed, healing can take place.

The use of individual therapies has its detractors. Regardless of their record of success for some people, the cost of long-term one-on-one therapy is high. Over a long period of time, these costs are beyond the reach of most Americans, especially the poor, who have been so harmed by the crack epidemic.

Group Therapy

Typically, the recovering addict participates in group therapy in addition to individual sessions with a therapist. Most cocaine therapists believe that at times in the recovery process addicts can learn valuable lessons from other recovering addicts. Groups generally consist of from three or four up to ten or fifteen addicts who are supervised by one therapist. Within the group setting, each addict has the opportunity not only to see how others deal with problems of addiction but to receive support and encouragement from other group members.

Group therapy sessions provide addicts with an opportunity to have their assumptions and excuses for their addictions challenged

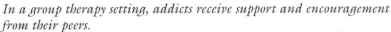

In a group therapy setting, addicts receive support and encouragement from their peers.

by their peers. This type of confrontational dialogue forces each member to maintain a high level of honesty with other group members. Whenever members believe that someone is lying or refusing to accept responsibility for his or her failures, they collectively challenge the person's comments and defenses. When this is done in a responsible manner, the confrontation forces the person to rethink whatever he or she said. In theory, addicts in this way can reach clearer insight into their behavior.

Under certain circumstances, group therapy may involve family and friends of the addict. Called intervention therapy, this treatment is generally used to motivate a cocaine addict to seek help or to take his or her addiction more seriously by forcing a confrontation with people who have the closest emotional ties with the addict. The theory behind intervention therapy is that family and friends can often motivate an addict more effectively than strangers can. Intervention therapy also educates the addict's family and friends about the problems of addiction and how to cope with the problems an addict may encounter while in therapy, such as loss of self-confidence, difficulty with communication, and feelings of guilt.

Medications

Although not commonly prescribed, for some patients medications are more effective than behavioral therapies. Two different types of medication are available. One causes intense discomfort if mixed with cocaine, and the other is used to help reduce the painful withdrawal symptoms and cravings during the first few weeks of abstinence.

Medications that create discomfort when mixed with cocaine are intended to deter addicts from using cocaine. The most common of these aversive drugs are Naltrexone and Clonidine. By themselves the medications are benign, but in combination with cocaine they elicit intense nausea and uncontrolled vomiting. Called aversion therapy because its goal is to create in the addict an aversion to the drug, the long-term goal is for the addict to abstain from using cocaine even though the benign medication that causes the nausea is no longer in his or her system.

The success of aversion therapy depends on the patient's compliance in taking the medication as prescribed. The pitfall, not surprisingly, is that some patients who crave the rush and euphoria of cocaine will stop taking the aversion drug because they simply want to enjoy their drug. Consequently, success with aversion therapy often requires that therapists monitor patients to ensure they are regularly taking their medicine.

A second medicinal therapy uses antidepressants such as Desipramine to control the depression that accompanies withdrawal from cocaine. The object of the medication is simply to reduce the pain of withdrawal and the likelihood that the addict will relapse. When this therapy works, doctors will gradually reduce the use of the antidepressant as the withdrawal symptoms lessen until none is needed.

Hope for the Future

Researchers at the Salk Institute in San Diego, California, are developing an entirely new approach for combating cocaine addiction called immunotherapy. Although it is still in the research stages, this approach involves using compounds that immunize addicts against the effects of cocaine. Immunotherapy aims to destroy the cocaine before it has any chance of reaching the brain in the first place. In essence, these compounds would work on cocaine the way antibodies do on microorganisms, rendering them harmless before they can reach the brain.

The lead investigator at the Salk Institute, Dr. Kim D. Janda, says, "We have created a new scientific approach for potential treatment of cocaine abuse and maybe drug abuse in general. We see a great deal of promise in this immunotherapy approach to drug treatment."[39] Dr. Donald Landry of Columbia University also sees promise for immunotherapy:

> Even if a cocaine blocker does not prevent every bit of the drug from reaching a user's brain, it may still act against addiction by blunting the intensity of the drug's high. The rush of smoking a large dose of crack might be reduced to the less overwhelming level of snorting a few milligrams of powdered cocaine. And that difference could be enough to start addicts on the road to recovery.[40]

A police officer hands out pins to first-graders as part of an antidrug education program.

In addition to medical research, many educational programs in schools, religious institutions, and clinics have had success deterring youngsters from using cocaine and other drugs. Many of the educational tools used in schools to discourage teenagers from using cocaine focus on a person's willpower or character strengths. The best deterrent to cocaine addiction, they propose, is for people to make choices that avoid contact with cocaine and cocaine users. Studies indicate that high school students actively involved in school sports, student government, honor societies, and church and community programs have a dramatically lower incidence of cocaine use than students who are uninvolved. Of greater significance, studies show that students involved in many activities rarely try cocaine—they have no interest. These studies lend support to the view that avoiding cocaine and addiction is a matter of being willing to make the right choices rather that being unable to do so.

Clinical studies of reformed cocaine addicts also show that if recovering cocaine addicts have meaningful activities in their lives such as jobs, families and friends, and spiritual affiliations, their chances of recovery increase. These studies, like those of high school students, support the view that it is a willingness to make the right choices that steers people clear of cocaine.

 **Epilogue**

Is the Cost of the War on Cocaine Justified?

Cocaine is a drug that will not go away. Since the 1970s, it has been a remarkably resilient opponent in America's war on drugs. Although cocaine use has declined from the highs of the 1980s, addiction rates have remained stable since 1991 and few new strategies have appeared to further reduce its presence in America. Deciding how best to proceed is complicated by mounting complaints from critics who question whether the limited results of America's war on cocaine justify the extremely high costs.

The monetary costs to the American taxpayers of the war against cocaine can only be estimated. The federal budget for all drug enforcement shows multiple allotments totaling about $25 billion annually, slightly more than half of which is spent seizing and controlling cocaine and crack. This figure, however, fails to take into account billions more spent by all branches of the military assisting in cocaine interdiction, or work performed by state and local police. A rough estimate of this additional money would be about $15 billion annually.

Critics argue that the cost is too high in view of the fact that most cocaine destined for the United States evades the complex web of governmental agencies charged with the responsibility of

Despite the billions of dollars spent on cocaine interdiction in the United States, approximately 90 percent of cocaine shipments evade detection.

seizing it. The DEA estimates that its agents seize about 10 percent of the one thousand tons shipped annually to the United States, which means the cost per ton is about $150 million. In contrast, the street price for a ton of cocaine in New York is approximately two-thirds that amount.

The DEA, however, counters the charges of critics by saying, "Drug control spending is a minor portion of the U.S. budget, and compared to the costs of drug abuse, spending is minuscule."[41] The cost of drug abuse, from the standpoint of the DEA as well as many Americans, is not measured in dollars but rather in the numbers of people whose lives are destroyed or damaged by the use of the drug.

In addition to lost and damaged lives, there is a financial as well as human toll exacted by the crimes associated with cocaine and crack trafficking. Thousands of people annually are injured by violent crimes perpetrated to get money for crack or to control the trafficking of the drug, and many of the most victimized are youngsters and women.

At this time, the consensus appears to be that the cost to continue the war against cocaine must be paid. A DEA spokesperson concludes, "We have made significant progress in reducing drug use in this country. Now is not the time to abandon our efforts." [42] Some Americans want to see more money spent on law enforcement, others want to see the money spent on treatment and prevention, while a minority wants to see cocaine legalized. The issues are complicated because they span many international borders and because they involve very large numbers of people and large amounts of money. Whatever path is taken, it is certain that cocaine will continue to be an issue for many years to come.

Notes

Chapter 1: A Once-Promising Drug

1. Quoted in BLTC Research website, www.cocaine.org/cocawine.htm.
2. Thomas Kosten, "Drug Addiction Treatment," in Electric Library website, www.sdcl.org.
3. R. I. Herning, D. E. King, W. Better, and J. L. Cadet, "Cocaine Dependence: A Clinical Syndrome Requiring Neuroprotection," *Annals of the New York Academy of Sciences,* vol. 846, June 1997, pp. 323–27.
4. Norbert R. Myslinski, "Addiction's Ugly Face," *World & I,* December 1, 1999, p. 166.
5. Quoted in National Institute on Drug Abuse website, www.nida.nih.gov/MedAdv/01/NR3-14.html. March 14, 2001.
6. Quoted in Gordon James Knowles, "Dealing Crack Cocaine: A View from the Streets of Honolulu," *FBI Law Enforcement Bulletin,* vol. 65, July 1, 1996, p. 1.
7. Quoted in Gilda Berger, *Crack: The New Drug Epidemic.* New York: Franklin Watts, 1987, p. 40.

Chapter 2: Illicit Use of Cocaine

8. Quoted in Stanford Online Report, "Alcohol, Tobacco Staples of Movies, Music, Study Finds," www.stanford.edu/dept/news/report/news/april28/movies-428-a.html.
9. Quoted in Joseph Spillane, "The Making of an Underground Market: Drug Selling in Chicago, 1900–1940," *Journal of Social History,* vol. 32, September 22, 1998, p. 27.
10. Quoted in Knowles, "Dealing Crack and Cocaine," p. 1.
11. Donald W. Landry, Tomo Narashima, and Johnny Johnson,

"Immunotherapy for Cocaine Addiction," *Scientific American,* vol. 276, February 1, 1997, p. 43.

12. Solomon Snyder, *Drugs and the Brain.* New York: Scientific American Books, 1986, p. 207.

13. James Lardner, "Criminals on Crime," *U.S. News & World Report,* vol. 124, May 25, 1998, p. 37.

14. Quoted in NIDA Notes, "31% of New York Murder Victims Had Cocaine in Their Bodies," by Neil Swan, vol. 10, no. 2, March/April 1995, http://165.112.78.61/NIDA_Notes/ NNVol10N2/Homicide.html.

Chapter 3: The Crack Epidemic

15. Quoted in Charles P. Cozic and Karin Swisher, *Chemical Dependency: Opposing Viewpoints.* San Diego: Greenhaven Press, 1991, p. 47.

16. U.S. Sentencing Commission, *Cocaine and Crime,* www. anaserve.com/~wethepeople/crime.htm.

17. U.S. Sentencing Commission, *Cocaine and Crime.*

18. U.S. Sentencing Commission, *Cocaine and Crime.*

19. David T. Courtwright, "The Drug War's Hidden Toll," *Issues in Science and Technology,* vol. 13, December 22, 1996, p. 72.

20. *Weekly Compilation of Presidential Documents,* "Interview with Jann Wenner of *Rolling Stone* Magazine," November 2, 2000, p. 301.

21. Jonathan Beaty, B. Russell Leavitt, and Janice C. Simpson, "Kids Who Sell Crack," *Time,* May 9, 1988, p. 20.

22. Berger, *Crack,* p. 32.

23. Quoted in Beaty, Leavitt, and Simpson, "Kids Who Sell Crack," p. 22.

Chapter 4: The Cocaine Partnership

24. Quoted in Juan Williams, "Analysis: Illegal Drug Trade and Inner Workings of a Cartel," Talk of the Nation, National Public Radio (NPR), October 4, 2000, radio interview.

25. Quoted in Claire Hargreaves, *Snowfields: The War on Cocaine in the Andes.* New York: Holmes & Meier, 1992, p. 35.

26. Quoted in Hargreaves, *Snowfields,* p. 38.
27. Quoted in Williams, "Analysis."
28. Quoted in Jan McGirk, "My Brother, Brilliant Villain of Medellín," *Independent,* January 2, 2001, p. 1.
29. Quoted in Linda Wertheimer, "New Cartel Taking Over Colombian Cocaine Trade," All Things Considered, National Public Radio (NPR), April 13, 1993.
30. U.S. Department of Justice, Drug Enforcement Administration, *The Supply of Illicit Drugs to the United States,* www. usdoj.gov/dea/pubs/intel/nnicc97.htm.

Chapter 5: Cocaine Interdiction

31. Quoted in Tom Fennell, Dominique Trottier, and Wilson Ruiz, "The Cocaine Fight: A Tale of Two Tactics," *Maclean's,* February 28, 2000, p. 30.
32. Quoted in Fennell, Trottier, and Ruiz, "The Cocaine Fight," p. 30.
33. *Economist,* "The Wages of Prohibition," December 24, 1994, p. 21.
34. Quoted at Drug Enforcement Administration website, *DEA Congressional Testimony,* www.usdoj.gov/dea/pubs/cngrtest/ ct021500.htm.
35. Quoted in Hargreaves, *Snowfields,* p. 188.

Chapter 6: Treatment and Recovery

36. *Drug Abuse: Research Shows Treatment Is Effective, but Benefits May Be Overstated.* Washington, DC: Government Accounting Office, April 27, 1998, p. 77.
37. Quoted in Patrick Zickler, *Combining Drug Counseling Methods Proves Effective in Treating Cocaine Addiction,* www.nida. nih.gov/NIDA_Notes/NNVol14N5/Combining.html.
38. Lewis R. Wolberg, *The Technique of Psychotherapy.* New York: Jason Aronson, 1995, p. 23.
39. Quoted in National Institute on Drug Abuse, NIDA Notes, March/April 1996, www.nida.nih.gov/NIDAHome.html.
40. Landry, Narashima, and Johnson, "Immunotherapy for Cocaine Addiction," p. 45.

Epilogue: Is the Cost of the War on Cocaine Justified?

41. Drug Enforcement Administration, "Speaking Out Against Drug Legalization," www.usdoj.gov/dea/demand/druglegal/index.html.

42. Drug Enforcement Administration, "Speaking Out Against Drug Legalization."

Organizations
to Contact

The Alliance Project
1954 University Ave. West, Suite 12
St. Paul, MN 55104
(651) 645-1618
e-mail: info@defeataddiction.org

The Alliance Project is a privately funded effort by a broad cross-section of organizations that share common concerns about the devastating disease of alcohol and drug addiction. The Alliance Project functions as a point of coordination and resource to organizations in the alcohol and drug addiction research, treatment, prevention, and especially the recovery communities.

Cocaine Anonymous
3470 Overland Ave.
Los Angeles, CA 90034
(310) 559-5833
website: www.ca.org/#home

Cocaine Anonymous is concerned solely with the personal recovery and continued sobriety of individual drug addicts. They offer a 12-step recovery program for addicts.

Drug Enforcement Administration (DEA)
2401 Jefferson Davis Hwy.
Alexandria, VA 22301
(202) 307-8846
website: www.usdoj.gov/dea/index.htm

The Drug Enforcement Administration website is maintained by the Department of Justice to provide the public with access to general information about the status of illegal drug use in the United States.

Narconon
1000 West Judo Rd.
Newkirk, OK 74647
(800) 468-6933
website: http://cocaineaddiction.com/index.html.

Narconon is a privately operated drug rehabilitation center that specializes in cocaine addiction and other drug addictions.

National Clearinghouse for Alcohol and Drug Information (NCADI)
11426-28 Rockville Pike, Suite 200
Rockville, MD 20852
(800) 729-6686
website: www.health.org/Index.htm

The National Clearinghouse for Alcohol and Drug Information is the information service of the Center for Substance Abuse Prevention of the Substance Abuse and Mental Health Services Administration in the U.S. Department of Health and Human Services. NCADI is the world's largest resource for current information and materials concerning substance abuse.

National Institute on Drug Abuse (NIDA)
6001 Executive Blvd., Room 5213
Bethesda, MD 20892-9651
(301) 443-1124
website: www.nida.nih.gov

The National Institute on Drug Abuse provides the latest information on drug abuse in America. Their information focuses on research information as well as statistics on drug use and focuses on warning the public of the risks involved with drug use.

The Substance Abuse and Mental Health Services Administration (SAMHSA)
5600 Fishers Ln.
Rockville, MD 20857
(301) 443-8956
website: www.samhsa.gov/

SAMHSA is the federal agency charged with improving the quality and availability of prevention, treatment, and rehabilitative services in order to reduce illness, death, disability, and cost to society resulting from substance abuse and mental illnesses.

For Further Reading

Gilda Berger, *Crack: The New Drug Epidemic*. New York: Franklin Watts, 1987. One of a very few books that provide nontechnical discussions about crack. Berger provides very good explanations about crack's origins, how it is made, how it affects the body, and its dangers. Also included in the book are interesting statistics on the crack industry and the politics of crack.

Mark S. Gold, *The 800-Cocaine Book of Drug and Alcohol Recovery*. New York: Villard Books, 1990. A survey of the variety of techniques and treatment available for cocaine and alcohol addiction. Gold presents a systematic guide for detoxification and long-term recovery. The book's value rests with the extraordinarily wide range of topics that are covered for those wishing to recover from habitual use or addiction.

Jennifer Lawler, *Drug Legalization*. Berkeley Heights, NJ: Enslow, 1999. Lawler's book focuses on several drug-related topics as well as the debate over whether illicit drugs should be legalized. She explores the history of illicit drugs, America's war on drugs, and insightful arguments, pro and con, for the legalization of illicit drugs in America.

Works Consulted

Books

Charles P. Cozic and Karin Swisher, eds., *Chemical Dependency: Opposing Viewpoints*. San Diego: Greenhaven Press, 1991. This anthology presents six controversial issues regarding drug dependency in a pro-con format. Many of the viewpoints presented are written by nationally recognized experts in the field of drug addiction.

Drug Abuse: Research Shows Treatment Is Effective, but Benefits May Be Overstated. Washington DC: Government Accounting Office, April 27, 1998.

Claire Hargreaves, *Snowfields: The War on Cocaine in the Andes*. New York: Holmes & Meier, 1992. One of the best accounts of the cocaine wars waged in the Andes. It includes first-person narratives by the peasants who grow the coca leaves and the accounts of the bosses of the cocaine cartels who control the processing and exporting. Hargreaves also describes the attempts on the part of the federal DEA to stop the exporting of cocaine and the Bolivian government officials who largely allow the cocaine operations to continue unchecked.

Eugene Richards, *Cocaine True, Cocaine Blue*. New York: Aperture, 1994. A combination of interviews and photographs of cocaine and crack addicts living in squalid conditions in New York City. Both the interviews and the photographs tell the story of drug addiction and the desperate lives of those addicted. The interviews provide stark insights into how these people survive and how they view their lives.

Solomon Snyder, *Drugs and the Brain*. New York: Scientific American Books, 1986. A short history of drug use and pharmacological research, organized according to major classes of psychoactive drugs.

Joseph F. Spillane, *Cocaine: From Medieval Marvel to Modern Menace in the United States, 1884–1920.* Baltimore: Johns Hopkins University Press, 2000. One of the very few histories of cocaine use in America during the early years of its introduction. This book provides statistics on early use, early perceptions for potential uses for cocaine, and how it was viewed by science and industry.

Robert Voy, *Drugs, Sports, and Politics.* Champaign, IL: Leisure Press, 1991. Focuses primarily on the history of cocaine use among both college and professional athletes. Voy discusses the role of cocaine in sports, the attitude of league owners toward the problem, and the reasons athletes risk using the drug. Includes a very good physiological discussion of how cocaine affects the body.

Lewis R. Wolberg, *The Technique of Psychotherapy.* New York: Jason Aronson, 1995. A highly technical reference book that focuses on the many techniques used in psychoanalysis.

Periodicals

Jonathan Beaty, B. Russell Leavitt, and Janice C. Simpson, "Kids Who Sell Crack," *Time*, May 9, 1988.

David T. Courtwright, "The Drug War's Hidden Toll," *Issues in Science and Technology*, vol. 13, December 22, 1996.

Economist, "The Wages of Prohibition," December 24, 1994.

Tom Fennell, Dominique Trottier, and Wilson Ruiz, "The Cocaine Fight: A Tale of Two Tactics," *Maclean's*, February 28, 2000.

Jack E. Henningfield, "Is Cocaine Addictive? It Depends on Whose Criteria You Use," *New York Times*, March 24, 1989.

R. I. Herning, D. E. King, W. Better, and J. L. Cadet, "Cocaine Dependence: A Clinical Syndrome Requiring Neuroprotection," *Annals of the New York Academy of Sciences*, vol. 846, June 1997.

Norman Kent, "Highwitness View," *High Times*, no. 154, July 1999.

Gordon James Knowles, "Dealing Crack Cocaine: A View from the Streets of Honolulu," *FBI Law Enforcement Bulletin*, vol. 65, July 1, 1996.

Donald W. Landry, Tomo Narashima, and Johnny Johnson, "Immunotherapy for Cocaine Addiction," *Scientific American,* vol. 276, February 1, 1997.

James Lardner, "Criminals on Crime," *U.S. News & World Report,* vol. 124, May 25, 1998.

Jan McGirk, "My Brother, Brilliant Villain of Medellín," *Independent,* January 2, 2001.

Norbert R. Myslinski, "Addiction's Ugly Face," *World & I,* December 1, 1999.

Yolanda Ruiz, "Kids and Crack," *Nation,* May 4, 1988.

Joseph Spillane, "The Making of an Underground Market: Drug Selling in Chicago, 1900–1940," *Journal of Social History,* vol. 32, September 22, 1998.

Weekly Compilation of Presidential Documents, "Interview with Jann Wenner of *Rolling Stone* Magazine," November 2, 2000.

David Williamson, "Breakthrough? Study Finds Dopamine Cannot Be Source of Pleasure in Brain," Carolina News Services, no. 155, March 13, 1999.

Teresa Wiltz, Diana Donnell, and Mia Mann, "Kicking Crack," *Essence,* vol. 26, April 1, 1996.

Radio

Bob Edwards, "Colombia Inundated with 28,000 Annual Murders," *Morning Edition,* National Public Radio (NPR), April 8, 1993.

Linda Wertheimer, "New Cartel Taking Over Colombian Cocaine Trade," All Things Considered, National Public Radio (NPR), April 13, 1993.

Juan Williams, "Analysis: Illegal Drug Trade and Inner Workings of a Cartel," Talk of the Nation, National Public Radio (NPR), October 4, 2000.

Websites

BLTC Research (www.bltc.com). BLTC Research is a British-based website predicting a utopian, "post-Darwinian" world of altered consciousness and permanent bliss through biotechnology. Content includes some factual information on the history and use of cocaine and other drugs.

Drug Enforcement Administration (DEA) (www.usdoj.gov/ dea/index.htm). The administration's website is maintained by the Department of Justice to provide the public with access to general information about the status of illegal drug use in the United States. The site includes statistics, discussions, publications, and other topics affecting the DEA.

Electric Library (www.sdcl.org). Maintained by the San Diego County Library, this website contains millions of full-text articles from a wide variety of periodicals.

Narconon (http://cocaineaddiction.com/index.html). Narconon is a drug rehabilitation center that specializes in cocaine addiction and other drug addictions. This website provides factual information about cocaine and crack and provides discussions about addiction and ideas about the best approaches to help addicts.

National Institute on Drug Abuse (NIDA) (www.nida.nih. gov/MedAdv/01/NR3-14.html). The institute provides the latest information on drug abuse in America. This website contains research reports as well as statistics on drug use and focuses on warning the public of the risks involved with drug use.

Schaffer Library of Drug Policy (www.druglibrary.org/schaffer/ index.HTM). An extensive database of articles, entirely of drug-related content. Articles address medical research, government policies, drug legalization debates, and health dangers. A valuable academic resource.

Stanford Online Report (www.stanford.edu). The Stanford Online Report is a university-wide website that disseminates information on the activities of all the departments at Stanford University.

U.S. Sentencing Commission (www.anaserve.com/~wethepeople/ crime.htm). Provides a database of hearings held by the U.S. Sentencing Commission. Full text of hearing transcripts can be accessed from this site.

Index

addiction
  cocaine, 20–22
  crack, 36–37
  cycle, 84
addicts
  female, 49
  harm reduction for, 82
  illnesses of, 47–49
  recovery of, 81
  stories of, 48
  treatment for
    group therapy, 87–88
    harm reduction, 82
    hope for future, 89–90
    immunotherapy, 89
    individual therapy, 85–87
    long-term, 81–83
    medications, 88–89
    multiple therapy strategy for, 84–85
    success of, 80–81
AIDS
  crack use and, 48–49
antidepressants, 89
antidrug education programs, 90
antisocial behavior, 31–33
athletes
  cocaine use by, 25
aversion therapy, 88–89

Beaty, Jonathan, 46
behavioral therapy, 84–86
Belenko, Steven, 41, 42
Bennett, Dolores, 47
Berger, Gilda, 46–47
Bias, Len, 26

Blaine, Jack, 85
brain chemistry
  cocaine addiction and, 20
  dopamine, 17, 27–29
  effects of cocaine on, 17–18, 29–30
  long-term damage to, 18–19

Cali cartel, 52
cardiovascular system
  effects of cocaine on, 16–17
  long-term damage to, 19
Cartagena cartel, 52
cartels
  bosses of, 55–56, 60–63, 70–71
  crop replacement thwarted by, 68
  distributors in, 57–60
  farmers in, 53–54
  manufacturers in, 54–57
  military assault on, 69–72
  organization of, 52–53
celebrities
  cocaine use by, 24–25
central nervous system
  effects of cocaine on, 17–18
  long-term damage to, 18–19
certification policy, 72
children
  cocaine use by, 66
  of crack addicts, 46, 47, 49
  crime and, 42–43
Clinton, Bill, 71
Clonidine, 88
Coca-Cola, 16
coca crops
  eradication of, 66–70

military assault on, 70
replacement of, 67–69
cocaine
  addiction cycle, 84
  addictive quality of, 20–22
  alkaloid, 11
  becomes illegal, 23–24
  commercial uses of, 15–16
  versus crack, 36–37
  crime and, 31–33
  dealers, 63–64, 76, 78–79
  early health claims for, 10–11
  effects of
    long-term
      physiological, 18–20
      psychological, 29–33
    short-term
      physiological, 16–18
      psychological, 27–29
  as energy booster, 10–11, 13–14,
    15–16
  epidemic, proposed solutions to, 9
  financial toll of, 8–9, 91–93
  human costs of, 7–8
  introduction of, in Europe, 13–14
  legalization of, 77
  manufacture of, 54–57
  medical uses of, 10–11, 13–15
  production
    efforts to reduce, 66–73
    stability of, 73–74
  psychosis, 29–33
  smuggling, 57–60, 63–64
  South American origins of, 11–12
  spread of, in 1970s, 6–7
  use of
    in 1970s, 24–26
    in 1980s, 26
  U.S. market for, 6
cocaine trade
  cartels
    bosses of, 55–56, 60–63, 70–71
    distributors in, 57–60
    farmers in, 53–54
    manufacturers in, 54–57
    organization of, 52–53

effects of, on South American
  economy, 50–52
interdiction of
  through crop eradication, 66–69
  by military assault, 69–72
  through seizures, 74–79
Cocaine True, Cocaine Blue
  (Richards), 31, 33, 39
coca leaves
  extraction of coca from, 54–55
  use of
    among Indian population, 11–12
    during Spanish conquest, 12–13
cocaleros, 53–54
Coca Wine, 11
cognitive therapy, 84, 86
coke bugs, 30, 31
Colombia
  cocaine-related violence in, 56
  foreign aid to, 72
  narco-terrorists in, 73
commercial products, 15–16
Courtwright, David T., 45
crack
  addictive quality of, 21, 35, 36–37
  babies, 7–8, 49
  versus cocaine, 36–37
  crime and, 41–45
  effects of
    on families, 45–47
    on inner cities, 37–41
  epidemic, 35–36
  houses, 37–38, 39
  introduction of, 7, 34–35
  legalization of, 77
  mandatory minimum sentencing
    and, 43–45
  manufacture of, 35
  potency of, 35
  related illnesses, 47–49
  rush from, 36
  violence over, 37
Crack: The New Drug Epidemic
  (Berger), 46–47
crime
  cocaine and, 31–33

crack-related, 7, 41–43
mandatory minimum sentencing
    for, 43–45
nonviolent, 31
youth and, 42–43
see also violence
cruceños, 60–63

dealers
organization of, 63–64
punishment of, 76, 78–79
deaths
cocaine-related, 23, 25–26
deception, 31
depression, 29, 30
distributors, 57–60
dopamine, 17, 27–29
drug cartels. *See* cartels
Drug Enforcement Administration
(DEA)
money spent by, 91–93
see also interdiction
drug traffickers, 63–64, 76, 78–79
drug treatment programs. *See*
treatment

economy
effects of cocaine trade on
    South America, 50–52
    United States, 8–9, 91–93
education programs
antidrug, 90
energy booster
cocaine as, 10–11, 13–14, 15–16
Erythoxylon coca, 11
Escobar, Pablo, 60, 61, 62, 70
Escobar, Roberto, 60
euphoria, 27–29
Europe
introduction of cocaine into,
    13–14

families
dysfunctional, 45–47
FARC (Revolutionary Armed
Forces of Colombia), 72, 73

farmers
eradication of coca crops and,
    66–69
as part of drug cartels, 53–54
Fennell, Tom, 68
foreign aid, 68–69, 72
Freud, Sigmund, 14, 15
Friedman, Milton, 77

Gilman, Benjamin, 73
group therapy, 85, 87–88

hallucinations, 30, 31
Hargreaves, Claire, 53
harm reduction, 82
health problems
See illness, crack-related
heart
damage to, 19
heart rate, 16–17
Henningfield, Jack E., 21
Herning, R.I., 19
High Intensity Drug Trafficking
Areas (HIDTA), 79
HIV
crack use and, 48–49
Hooker, William, 13
human costs, 7–8

illness
crack-related, 47–49
immunotherapy, 89
inner cities
crack and, 37–41
interdiction, 65–79
border seizures, 74–76
certification policy, 72
crop replacement, 67–69
domestic seizures, 78–79
eradication of coca crops,
    66–69
failures of, 73–74, 76
financial costs of, 91–93
military assaults, 69–72
success of, 65, 75
intervention therapy, 88

Janda, Kim D., 89

Kingpin Act, 76
Kosten, Thomas, 18

Landry, Donald W., 28–29, 89
Lardner, James, 31–32
law enforcement measures,
   65–79
   border seizures, 74–76
   certification policy, 72
   against crack addicts/dealers, 38,
      40
   domestic seizures, 76, 78–79
   eradication of coca crops, 66–69
   failures of, 73–74, 76
   financial costs of, 91–93
   military assaults, 69–72
   success of, 65, 75
Ledwith, William, 75–76
legalization, 77
Leshner, Alan I., 20

mandatory minimum sentences,
   43–45, 76
manufacturers, 54–57
Medellín cartel, 52, 58–59, 70
medical applications, 10–11, 13–15
medications, 88–89
Mexico, 63
military assaults, 69–72
Mobile Enforcement Team (MET),
   79
monetary costs, 91–93
movie industry,
   portrayal of cocaine by, 25
Myslinksi, Norbert R., 20

Naltrexone, 88
Narconon, 99
narco-terrorists, 73
National Clearinghouse for Alcohol
   and Drug Information (NCADI),
   99
National Household Survey on
   Drug Abuse (NHSDA), 40, 65

National Institute on Drug Abuse
   (NIDA), 33, 99
National Narcotics Intelligence
   Consumers Committee (NNICC),
   63
neurotransmitters, 17, 27–29

Operations Pipeline and Convoy, 79

pain relief, 11, 12, 13
paranoia, 30
Pastrana, Andres, 71
physiological effects. See cocaine,
   effects of
pichicateros, 54
positron emission tomography
   (PET), 18–19
poverty
   cocaine trade as escape from
      for South American peasants,
         50–52, 54
   crack use and, 46–47
   prostitution, 49
psychological effects. See cocaine,
   effects of
psychotherapy, 84, 86

racial issues
   crack and, 38, 40, 45
recovery. See treatment
rehabilitation. See treatment
Revolutionary Armed Forces of
   Colombia (FARC), 72, 73
Richards, Eugene, 31, 33, 39
Roberts, Donald F., 25
rush, 27–29
Ryan, Elisabeth, 36–37

self-deception, 31
serotonin, 17
smuggling
   by aircraft, 58–59, 75
   border seizures and, 74–76
   domestic, 63–64
   methods of, 57–60
   Mexico's role in, 63

Snowfields (Hargreaves), 53
Snyder, Solomon, 29
South America
　cocaine-related violence in, 56, 67
　effects of cocaine trade on
　　economy of, 50–52
　foreign aid to, 68–69, 72
　narco-terrorists in, 73
　origins of cocaine in, 11–12
strokes, 19
Szasz, Thomas, 77

tachycardia, 19
therapy. *See* treatment
treatment
　cost of, 9
　group therapy, 87–88
　harm reduction, 82
　hope for future, 89–90
　immunotherapy, 89
　individual therapy, 85–87
　long-term, 81–83
　medications, 88–89
　multiple therapy strategy, 84–85
　success of, 80–81

Über Coca (Freud), 15
United States
　cocaine market, 6, 63–64
　customs officials

　　border seizures by, 74–76
　　bribery of officials in, 59
　　smuggling and, 57–60
　effects of cocaine trade on
　　economy of, 8–9, 91–93
urban poor
　crack and, 7–8

ventricular fibrillation, 19
Vin Mariani, 15–16
violence
　cocaine use and, 31–33
　in Colombia, 56
　crack epidemic and, 7, 37, 41–43
　in South America, 61, 67
　victims of, 33
　see also crime

Welna, David, 56, 62
Wenner, Jann, 45
Wightman, R. Mark, 17
Wilhelm, Charles E., 73
Wolberg, Lewis R., 86

youth
　cocaine use among, 66
　crack-related crime among,
　　42–43

zepes, 54

Picture Credits

About the Author

James Barter received his undergraduate degree in history and classics at the University of California (Berkeley) followed by graduate studies in ancient history and archaeology at the University of Pennsylvania. Mr. Barter has taught history as well as Latin and Greek.

A Fulbright scholar at the American Academy in Rome, Mr. Barter worked on archaeological sites in and around the city as well as on sites in the Naples area. He also has worked and traveled extensively in Greece.

Mr. Barter currently lives in Rancho Santa Fe, California, with his fifteen-year-old daugher Kalista who enjoys soccer, the piano, and mathematics. His older daughter, Tiffany Modell, also lives in Rancho Santa Fe and works as a violin teacher and music consultant.